Your Successful Project Management Career

Your Successful Project Management Career

Ronald B. Cagle

AMACOM
American Management Association
New York • Atlanta • Brussels • Chicago • Mexico City • San Francisco
Shanghai • Tokyo • Toronto • Washington, D.C.

Special discounts on bulk quantities of AMACOM books are available to corporations, professional associations, and other organizations. For details, contact Special Sales Department, AMACOM, a division of American Management Association, 1601 Broadway, New York, NY 10019.
Tel.: 212-903-8316. Fax: 212-903-8083.
Web site: www.amacombooks.org

Library of Congress Cataloging-in-Publication Data

Cagle, Ronald B.
Your successful project management career / Ronald B. Cagle.
p. cm.
Includes bibliographical references and index.
ISBN 0-8144-0824-9
1. Project management. 2. Project management—Vocational guidance. I. Title.

HD69.P75C3453 2005
658.4'04—dc22 *2004009923*

Printing number

10 9 8 7 6 5 4 3 2 1

Contents

Preface

Project management is a hot topic. It is a hot topic because projects are the nerve center of a company. It is where new products come from and it's where profits are made or lost. In simplest terms, companies live or die based on the success of their projects. The single most important element in a project's success is the leadership of the project manager. But what is a project manager? Look at the Job Opportunities pages, and what do you see?

Project Manager
E-Marketing Project Manager
Peoplesoft Project Manager—financials
Facilities Project Manager
Program Manager Simulation and Modeling
Project Mgr—IT Finance/BA
Logistics Engineer/Project Manager
MMS Project Manager
Project Manager/Business Analyst
IT Analysis Project Managers
Telecom Network Project Managers
Construction Project Manager
Program Manager

It may prompt you to ask: "What in the world is an IT Analysis Project Manager?" "Who is a Telecom Network Project Manager?" And: "How are they different from a Project Manager?" All good questions! This book will answer these questions and a whole lot more. I will talk about Project Managers and Telecom Project Managers as well as others and project management and program management and show how they all relate to each other. Project management is not a binary issue; it is an issue with many variables and many requirements.

We will start with a "big picture" view of project management. How it started, how it developed, and where it is now. We'll explore who the movers and shakers are and what all this means to you.

There's a lot of detail in this book. But, even with all the detail, you may need to do some interpolation to find exactly where you stand in all this. The book is also broad. But even with its breadth, you may need to do some extrapolation to create a direction for yourself that will meet your long-term goals. But, after all, interpolation and extrapolation are a big part of project management. It is not simple and straightforward and must be treated as a complex subject

Contrary to what you may have been led to believe, project management is not a simple "Read a book, take a test, and you can do it" exercise. The field of project management is a broad and deep sea where you will create your own course based on your own long-term objectives. Fortunately, there are some lighthouses and buoys along the way, and I will point them out to you to help you stay in the channel.

Part I sets the scene. I explain what project management is all about, where it came from, and where it is today, and introduce you to the various organizations that are the guideposts of the project management discipline. Then I help you determine which organization is right for you. Part I also defines the terms used in project management and separates the different project types. It defines the skill sets and leadership roles required to lead the different project types. Finally, it compares the project types, the skill sets, and the leadership roles.

Part II introduces the five skill set levels and concentrates on achieving these skill levels. The subject areas that constitute each skill level are then presented. Here is where the detail sets in. Each skill level is explained, and I show you a path to achieve each one.

Part III concentrates on improving your project management abilities by allowing you to assess your capabilities. Then I recommend ways to expand your knowledge, gain experience, develop your persona, and improve your performance. If you are looking forward to what you can do with what you have or with what you will develop, this is the chapter that will help you.

Part IV compares the skill levels to various projects and programs and shows you why the different skill levels are important.

Part V is about making career moves at different times in your career and for different reasons. Now that you have it all together, what are you going to do with it? This part talks about the advantages of staying where you are versus moving to another department or company, and if you move, what you can expect when you get there.

Part VI advocates that you keep the momentum going. Project management is a dynamic discipline, and you really need to stay on top of it. New ideas, new software, and new approaches are being developed every day. I have included recommendations for staying on top of all of these.

You may have noticed that I refer to project management as a discipline and not a profession. What do I mean by this? My view is this: Engineering is a profession, electrical engineering is a discipline. Accounting is a profession, cost accounting is a discipline. Management is a profession, project management is a discipline. So, project management is really a part of the overall profession of management. In fact, project management is the bridge between all the staff elements of the company and the technical heart of the company. To really understand project management, consider it an appliqué—an overlay, if you will—of the entire project task. Project management is, in fact, one of the disciplines that contributes to the overall task by providing planning and leadership. This is fundamental to the concept of the project team.

On the basis of my experience and research I have identified five levels of project and program management. My objective in creating these levels is to set out a plan that coincides with the way business looks at project and program managers. In other words, how business hires, assigns, and promotes project managers—their most important resource. My categorizations differ from those set out by the leading project management organizations, but that's just because there are different reasons for the categories we have each created.

As I said before, you don't read a book or take a course or take a test and wake up some morning as a project manager, nor are you a project manager because your boss appoints you as one. Project management is a discipline you grow into a little at a time. Why? Because project performance holds the purse strings of the company, and project performance is based on the performance of the project manager. No responsible company management will trust an individual with leading a large project or program until they are certain the person has the right stuff.

Individuals grow into project management from their technical fields. Technical fields include computer science, engineering, finance, banking, health, construction, and dozens of others. Whatever they are, those are the technical fields to which I refer. Individuals can grow into the project management field, but not before they show they are capable of being a manager at some level. Individuals become project managers by first gaining knowledge, then by applying that knowledge to gain experience. Through it all they develop a persona. All this is applied to a task (a project) that results in a performance. If the performance is positive, there will be success. If performance is not positive, the project manager will be looking for another job.

I have devised a table to show you why I have chosen to categorize projects into seven levels and project managers into five levels. Notice that at each complexity level the project manager's technical task becomes smaller and the management task becomes larger. The percentages are devised to show relativity; they are not absolutes. In the far right column is a reference to a PM Skill Level. These levels are explained in detail as the book unfolds. Suffice it to say at this point that the qualifications for each level grow from top to bottom in the table. Certainly it is understandable that responsible management assigns project or program leadership based on the individual's competence.

Project management is not a simple discipline. In fact, it is one of the most complex and difficult jobs in the company. The only way you can maintain your position as a project manager is through positive performance. But positive performance doesn't just happen, it is a complex process that begins with knowledge, is compounded by experience, and is vectored by persona.

Over the years, I have developed a formula that expresses success in project management. This formula is:

Knowledge + Experience + Persona × Performance = Success

Notice the arithmetic factors in the formula. The factors say that Knowledge and Experience and Persona are additive factors but that Performance is a multiplier. Therefore it is much more important than the other factors. The interesting thing though is that you really can't have positive performance without the other factors. In the formula all factors are interdependent. The formula treats knowledge as the leverage that allows you to gain information quickly. It treats experience as the opportunity that allows you to apply that knowledge, and it treats your persona as the vector you will use to apply your knowledge and gain experience. With all these factors working in concert, you end up with positive performance. With positive performance, you have success.

Throughout this book there are references to other books and articles. In addition, there are references to many Web sites. When perusing these references, you should keep these things in mind: Printed material is a matter of history. It takes time to formulate and print a book, and, to a lesser extent, an article. Consequently, the timelines of printed material are somewhat dated. But, once printed, the book or article is, at least theoretically, always available. Web sites, on the other hand, usually contain current and dynamic data and can change overnight. Information that is available today may or may not be available tomorrow or it may be available in a different place. This means that as you use the references of this book, you are pretty well assured that a book or article reference will be available but the data may be somewhat dated. The references to Web sites will probably be current but the sites may or may not exist because they may have been updated or removed.

Acknowledgments

I am indeed fortunate to have many friends and associates who are program managers and project managers. The experience of each one is a little different, and each of them is an expert in his or her own field. As this book drew to a close, I asked several of them to participate in a peer review of the manuscript so that you, the reader, could experience the best-of-the-best. I was fortunate to have three such individuals take time from their busy schedules to read and comment on the manuscript. Their comments have been invaluable.

Mr. Robert Gray—Bob has more than thirty years of experience with leading-edge technology, specializing in program management, business development, and software engineering. He has had an excellent performance with regard to profit, division staffing, technical quality, cost, and schedule on commercial and government contracts, including both firm fixed price and cost plus. Bob has been recommended for the Phoenix Award (the highest program turnaround award in program management).

Ms. Carolyn Plank, PMP—Carolyn has more than fifteen years' experience as a project manager in the computer industry. She is a technology manager for a multinational computer hardware, software, and services company. She has extensive background in software development, international project management, training, and consulting. She achieved her PMP certification in 1995 and is a longtime member of the Project Management Institute (PMI). She is a founding member of the PMI Space Coast, Florida Chapter, and is currently on the chapter's Board of Directors.

Mr. James Staal—Jim is a Certified Business and Executive Coach and owns Azure Group, Inc., which provides consulting and coaching in management and technical areas. Their motto is: "Working with businesses and people to turn Dreams into Visions and Visions into Reality." Jim spent many years as a program manager and system engineer with computer and aerospace companies.

My wife, Judy, is a teacher and was my "sounding board" throughout the preparation of this manuscript. Her comments regarding structure and composition were invaluable and her putting up with my being on the computer day and night will most certainly nominate her for sainthood.

To each and all of you, my thanks.

PART I

UNDERSTANDING PROJECT MANAGEMENT TODAY

Project management is a logical technique, and, as such, has been with us for centuries, whether we recognize it not. Project management is the methodology used to control task, schedule, and cost of a project.

Project management methodology was probably used to build the pyramids and may have even been used before that, if only we had evidence of accomplishments to prove it.

The methodology persisted in rudimentary form until about 1950, when it became evident that something more comprehensive was necessary to cope with the ever-increasing sophistication of projects. Because we were building complicated electromechanical systems and planning to send rockets to the moon and beyond, the U.S. federal government sought a protocol that would result in reports that could be checked periodically to ensure a task was on track.

Just such a protocol emerged from the design process of the Polaris missile program. The Polaris missile program was extremely complex and involved many, many subcontractors as well as thousands of parts.

To top it all off, the program was on a very demanding timeline. Once again, the ingenuity of man came to the rescue, and a new protocol was developed. That protocol is known as the Program Evaluation and Review Technique (PERT) and was developed on a contract with the U.S. Navy. About the same time, industry created a scheduling process now known as the Critical Path Method (CPM). The CPM has been the basis for nearly all the scheduling and work processing methodologies that followed. PERT and CPM are now used jointly, and you may see them titled as PERT/CPM. Once you have all the information necessary for PERT, it is relatively easy to look for the minimum timeline within all the activities. This minimum timeline is the Critical Path. In both these techniques, you divide the elements of the project into smaller and smaller activities and then place those activities into a network that represents the overall project. Dividing cost into smaller and smaller activities allows more precise control of the overall project. Dividing the task into smaller elements allows more exacting control over the specification and requirements for the final product.

But those techniques were just the start of a process that would grow in depth and breadth over time. And, as the process grows, we need to train people in the use of the techniques to control actual projects and educate them to expand the discipline. As this book unfolds, you will see just how complex project management is today. You will see the training, education, and experience you will need to become a project manager, proficient at the various levels of projects and programs that exist within the discipline today.

CHAPTER 1

Understanding What Project Management Is All About

Let's start by establishing some definitions, so we are all on the same page. The first is: "Projects and Programs." Here, we will look at the structure of projects and programs and what they are all about. Then we will go through the various stages and phases that constitute projects and programs. Next comes: "The Project Management Process." An understanding of what the project management process is all about is essential to understanding how the project manager applies his or her talents to conducting projects and programs. Then: "The Portability of the Process." Just how applicable is the project management process to all the disciplines, and can you take it with you? Next, "The Project Manager." Since you may have a definition of this term that you got from another book or you may have a definition unique to your organization, I will give my definition, so it is clear as you read this book. Next, we will look at the requirements for becoming a project manager. Then, we will introduce the "Path to Success." Finally, the all-important issue: "Deciding if Project Management Is for You." The equation applied to this decision will guide *Your Successful Project Management Career*.

Projects and Programs

The purpose of both projects and programs is to produce a product or service, or both, according to a requirement, by some moment in time, for a certain cost. A project is performed for an in-house customer; a program is performed for an out-of-house customer under the aegis of a legal contract. In order to accomplish this, a requirement is developed (hopefully written) and assigned to a group for execution. The group, led by a project or program manager, plans how they will perform the task and documents the plan. Then, they go about executing the plan.

Finally, when the task is completed, the project or program is closed, and the product is transferred to the originator of the requirement.

Figure 1-1 shows the steps necessary to get from the requirement to the product or service. For the sake of commonality and control, projects and programs are first divided into stages and then into phases to show needs, actions, and accomplishments. A rough standard has evolved to portray this relationship. I say "rough" because terminology changes with the person telling the story and the viewpoint from which the story is told. Regardless of what the stages or phases are called, the relationship remains the same. Each part of the portrayal has an identifier so that you can keep up with what's going on. Figure 1-1 shows the relationship of the identifiers in a linear fashion by showing the parts called stages and the parts called phases.

The four stages constitute the "big picture." To lay some groundwork, let's start by describing what happens in each of the stages. You can get a feel for when each of the stages starts and finishes by looking at Figure 1-2.

Because a program is responsive to a legal contract between the performing organization and the requiring organization, the Initiating Stage is somewhat different in a program than in a project. In projects, the Initiating Stage is accomplished within the company although it may be in a different section, division, or group than the performing organization. The customer develops and documents the requirement and hands it over to the performing organization. In a program, the Initiating Stage is accomplished by a customer outside the performing company. The customer develops a requirement that is usually competitively bid, negotiated, and then awarded to the performing organization under the aegis of a contract. In a program, the Initiating Stage is

Figure 1-1. Relationship between the stages and phases.

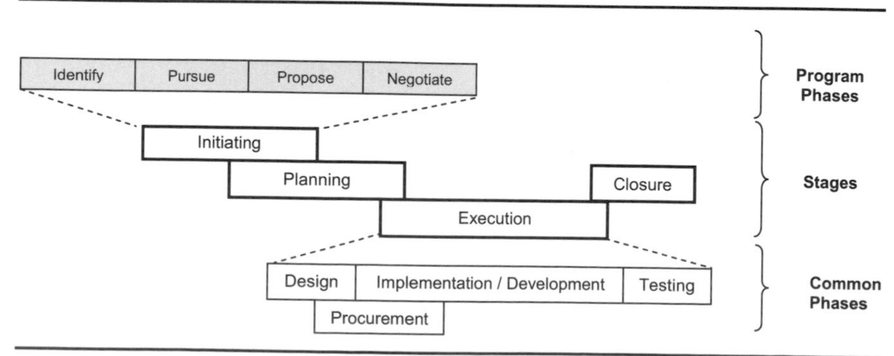

Figure 1-2. Project and program stages.

Stage	
A time in the project or program in which specific activities dominate. (There is some amount of overlap between stages.)	
Initiating Stage	Begins when a project is initiated or a program is identified, includes the proposal and ends with award.
Planning Stage	Begins at or before award and ends with kickoff.
Execution Stage	Begins with kickoff and ends at the completion of final test.
Closure Stage	Begins at the start of the final test and ends with total completion of the project or program.

divided into several phases, but these phases overlap considerably. For instance, making teaming agreements and alliances as well as developing the proposal are overlapping parts of the pursuit phase.

The Planning and Closure Stages are divided more by events than by discrete phases. The Planning Stage includes developing the program plan, selecting and training the personnel, and presenting the kickoff meeting. These events are usually not separated because they overlap so much. Further, the sequence is inconsistent. Usually, the project manager creates an action list that shows the start and finish of the separate events and the actions contained in each. The action list is posted to allow the team to see each day's activities.

The Execution Stage is the very heart of both the project and the program, and because of its complexity and duration, is divided into several phases. Figure 1-3 contains the actions that are contained in each of the phases. As you can see in Figure 1-1, the common phases are contained solely within the Execution Stage.

Note: When you read through the PMI PMBOK (part of the recommended reading for the Basic Skill Set in Chapter 6) you will find that the Project Management Institute (PMI) chooses to use the term *processes* rather than *stages*. PMI calls these processes: Initiating, Planning, Executing, and Closing. Just like the stages in Figure 1-1. In the PMI depiction, "Controlling" processes overlay all the other processes. In truth, they are both processes and stages. I chose to use the term *stages* here because, if we don't, we get into a compounding of the term *processes*.

Figure 1-3. Project and program phases.

Phase	
A time in the project or program in which specific efforts dominate.	
Design Phase	The phase in which the product or system is designed. Begins with the concept and ends with the final design review. Includes the definition and sometimes the design of subassemblies.
Procurement Phase	The phase in which subassemblies and components are procured. This phase may include the issue, performance, and closure of subcontracts.
Implementation Phase	The phase in which the assemblies and subassemblies are brought together to form a hardware system or computer program.
Development Phase	The phase in which a product or computer program is brought together and "grown" into the final product or computer program.
Testing Phase	The phase in which all tests are performed. The recognized testing phase usually includes assembly tests and final tests. Component tests and subassembly tests are usually a part of subcontracts or purchases.
O&M Phase	The phase in which the system or product is operated and maintained. Indeed, it is probably the reason it was developed in the first place. The Operations Phase or Operations and Maintenance Phase may or may not be part of a project or program task statement.

The Project Management Process

By my definition, the project management process consists of the sum of the processes, the stages, and the phases; therefore, the Project Management Process (singular) is the effective control of all the factors during the stages and the phases of a project or program from beginning to end.

The Applicability of the Project Management Process

The project management process is essentially applicable to all industries, disciplines, companies, and jobs. However, in a lot of documentation you will see the phrase: "The Portability of the Process." The statement goes on to say that the process is portable from job to job, industry to industry, and company to company. Even though that statement is true on the surface, the inference many people draw from this statement is that if you are a project manager in one discipline, let's say pharmaceuticals, you can move to another industry, let's say aerospace, and lead a program there. This is *not* true. Even though the concepts are portable from industry to industry, and so on, the details are not. The reason is that the project manager must be critically attuned to the technical details of the projects he or she is leading in order for the project to be successful. For this reason, I use the term "The Applicability of the Project Management Process."

The Project Manager

The most general definition of a project manager is a person who employs the project management process. Although you can argue with this definition, and I do, it is the way the term is used throughout most of the commercial world today. Why? Because it makes people feel better and makes the job appear more important if the term "manager" is used. Frankly, that definition is oversimplified. In truth, a project manager is, or should be, one who manages projects—that is, he or she has the authority to truly manage the project by moving resources around and into and out of the project. A little further in the book, the terms supervisor and manager will be introduced. Even further, when the different project sizes are introduced, the definition will be compounded. When you start looking for a new position, it is up to you to use all the definitions in this chapter and decide whether the position you seek is really a project manager, or if it is a project coordinator, or a project supervisor that is called a project manager. There's nothing wrong with calling a coordinator or a supervisor a manager so long as you understand what the job is all about.

There are three skill groups a project manager must have in order to be effective: a technical skills group, a project management skills group, and a people skills group (a skill group is different from a skill set, which you will see later). First, the project manager must know what the task is all about from a technical standpoint. For that reason, we frequently see advertisements for: IT strategy project managers, or construction project managers, or the like. Needless to say, the technical tasks these two project managers must lead are dramatically different. Consequently, each must possess a different technical skill in order to perform the specific task assigned. Second, a project manager must possess project management skills—that is, the ability to create schedules and budgets, the ability to implement and manage change control systems, the ability to implement and manage risk management systems, and the ability to implement and manage the many other project management skills as well. These are frequently referred to as the "Hard" (I prefer the term "Firm") project management skills. Third, a project manager must possess the so-called "Soft" skills. These skills are frequently called the people skills. The Australian Institute of Project Management (AIPM) presents an excellent summary of these skills.[1] They stipulate that a project manager possess these characteristics:

- Leadership ability
- The ability to anticipate problems
- Operational flexibility
- The ability to get things done
- An ability to negotiate and persuade
- An understanding of the environment within which the project is being managed
- The ability to review, monitor, and control
- The ability to manage within an environment of constant change

While all these skills do contain a certain amount of firm knowledge, they depend on the personal characteristics of the project manager to apply them properly. They are absolutely necessary to successfully lead a project composed of more than a single discipline and more than a few people.

The abilities that a project or program manager must possess will vary with the numbers of people, the value, the technical content, and the legal content of the project or program. Consequently, the abilities of the project or program manager need to be "matched" to the role to be performed without going overboard.

- Projects or programs with large numbers of people need a manager who understands the needs of people and of organizing them to get the job done. They don't need an on-site psychologist.

- Projects or programs of high dollar value need a manager with administrative (budgeting and scheduling) skills but he or she must avoid being so involved with the process that the other issues of the task are ignored (commonly called "paralysis by analysis").
- Projects or programs of high technical content need a manager who understands all the disciplines included in the project, but he or she must avoid being so involved in the technical design or technical issues that the project management and people issues are ignored.
- Programs with legal content need a manager who understands legal issues but not an on-site lawyer.

All projects or programs require a manager who has the most important ability of all: leadership. "Leadership is influence, nothing more, nothing less.[2]

Now, what does all this mean to you and why should it be in such a prominent position in the book? It means that, when you are applying for a job or a new position as project manager, you must make sure the job is a correct fit for you, your abilities, and even your personality. If you are a qualified and experienced project manager and are offered a job with another company, ensure the job is what you want it to be and what you need it to be or that you can shape it into what you want it to be.

Suppose you are accustomed to moving resources around on your jobs and signing off on subcontracts and materials. In other words, having complete latitude in making your project work. If your new job does not allow you the same latitude, you may be in for a lot of frustration, even if you are making more money. This can be injurious to your career. I had a personal experience with this condition, and it was frustrating. In my case, everything went well until the last interview, when the cat came out of the bag. At the last moment, my interviewer said I would be reporting to a level different from the one we had been discussing all along. Did I have any problem with that? I said, "Yes, I do have a problem with that." And that was the end of it. I found that the president of the area I was supposed to be in didn't want my position reporting to someone else. I was fortunate enough to see the handwriting on the wall and declined the position.

Suppose you are offered a position that is within your capabilities, and everything looks great. In fact, everything is too great. During negotiations you double your present salary, and the interviewer doesn't even blink. You request some heavy-duty requirements such as an extended household move, and still the interviewer doesn't even blink. Something is not quite right here. This happened to me once. Fortunately, I had enough contacts to find out that the program I was to take over was a disaster, and there was just no way anyone could revive it. I found that they were looking for someone to blame for the failure. I turned that position down as well.

Suppose you have very limited experience in running projects and you are offered a job allowing you complete latitude to change resources, and so on. You are then responsible for the results. To accept this job could mean that you are in over your head and destined for failure. Certainly, this will hurt your career. Granted, you should always extend yourself or you will never grow. But, be certain that desire, extra-achievable training, and hard work will make up the difference and you can emerge from the project positively.

As you can see, a project manager is a complex person with a multiplicity of skills. Projects that vary in size, value, and complexity require project managers with different skill sets. These skill sets are not gained overnight, they are part of a learning process that takes a long time—sometimes years. As you read on through this book, you will see the several different skill sets necessary to lead the different project and program types. In the case of project managers, one size does not fit all!

The Path to Success

The path to success can be expressed in a very simple formula. Achieving success, however, is not quite so simple. The path to success is:

Knowledge + Experience + Persona × Performance = Success

Knowledge is a combination of both education and training. Experience is the application of that knowledge. Persona is the personality and attitude you project to your team members, your management, and your customer. Finally, performance is how well it all comes together and how the product turns out, how satisfied management is, and how satisfied the customer is. Performance is the most important factor, because no matter how great each and every one of the other factors is, if performance did not create the product the customer specified or did not provide the profit level that management established, performance will be less than desired, and the project will have been a failure.

We will be referring to the Path to Success at a number of points in this book.

Deciding if Project Management Is for You

If you're like everyone else when making decisions that will affect your career, you want to know: what, where, when, why, and how. I hope to answer as many of these questions for you as I can.

So far, we've talked about the fact that project management is a hot topic, and it's a hot topic because it controls the projects that provide the lifeblood of the company. Now is the time to start laying the groundwork so you can make an informed decision.

My job is to present as much information as possible for you to determine if you want to be a project manager, and if so, at what level. I will begin that process by talking about the organizations through which you can network to meet people and hiring organizations and even job opportunities. Furthermore, these organizations can provide reference materials and paths to certification.

It is a good idea to be able to "talk the talk," so I've included a glossary at the end of the book. It contains the terms used in the book and the terms that will be thrown at you in the project management world.

Next, we will get into the detailed skill sets that are necessary to achieve the several levels of project and program management. No doubt you will want to improve your abilities to achieve further levels, so I'll provide a chapter that concentrates on this information. Gathering information is one thing but applying it is quite another. The book provides a part that outlines how these skills you worked so hard for can be applied at the different project levels. Then we will talk about applying those skills to projects of different sizes. At this point you may well want to advance your own career by quantum leaps rather than small steps. You can do this by viewing potential areas within your company that need project managers of your advanced standing or by changing companies. We'll go through the details of how to handle these changes before and after you make your moves.

Finally, you will find that project management is a constantly changing discipline. We will look at where project management is going and the personal advancements you need to keep up with the "bow wave." Let's get started.

Notes

1. Australian Institute of Project Management, *National Competency Standards for Project Management*, Vol. 1 (Yeronga, QLD: AIPM, 1996): 19.
2. John C. Maxwell, *The 21 Irrefutable Laws of Leadership* (Nashville, Tenn.: Thomas Nelson Publishers, 1998).

CHAPTER 2

Introducing the Principal Organizations

The "movers and shakers" are pretty clear at this point. In Australia, it is the Australian Institute for Project Management (AIPM); in Great Britain, the Association for Project Management (APM) is the recognized leader; the International Project Management Association (IPMA) sets standards for participating organizations all over the world. In the United States and many countries throughout the world, it is the Project Management Institute (PMI).

In addition to these project management organizations, the American Management Association (AMA) is a leader in providing management books and seminars. Project management is a part of their management coverage, and the AMA is therefore an excellent source for project management information.

As you might expect, the movers and shakers are the ones who establish the standards and bodies of knowledge and certification processes for their sphere of influence. In some cases, these spheres of influence overlap. When they do overlap, several things happen. First, there is competition between the two for new members. Second, there is competition between the two for dominance. Dominance, in this case, means whose standards and whose doctrine will be used for the now-disputed members and area. Third, can and will they coexist?

Generally speaking, development and proliferation of the organizations has been on a geographical basis. Each country has its own requirements for qualification and certification (more on that later). The Project Management Institute (PMI) has defied that mold somewhat and now reportedly has over 100,000 members in more than 125 countries. Even though the PMI is recognized worldwide and offers its certification worldwide, the PMI does not offer a specific international certification as does the APM.

To get a feel of how all of this has come about, over time, consider Figure 2-1. It shows that the PMI was the first to recognize the need for a formal project management process. It also shows that the Australian standards were modified by the incorporation of the PMI's PMBOK in 1995, which leads to some degree of commonality. You can see by the dates that project management, as a discipline, has been around for a while, but in the late 1980s and 1990s took a giant leap. Interest and standardization are increasing rapidly. The British APM took a bold leap forward in 1998 and was the driving force to create an international group for project management, the International Project Management Association (IPMA). The IPMA is a worldwide organization and is the first real step toward international standardization of at least the core issues. There are now many countries where the PMI and IPMA as well as local standards exist.

To try to make your contact with the appropriate organization a little easier, the data in Figure 2-2 provides a list of project management organizations. Contact details will be provided in the following paragraphs.

Figure 2-1. Chronology of Project Management Association and documentation development.

ORG	ACTION	1969	1976	1977	1988	1989	1995	1996	1998	1999
PMI	PMI formed	X								
AIPM	AIPM formed		X							
AIPM	AIPM issues NCSPM			X						
PMI	PMI issues PMBOK				X					
APM	APM formed (?)				X					
APM	PRINCE developed					X				
AIPM	AIPM incorporates PMI PMBOK						X			
APM	PRINCE2 developed							X		
IPMA	IPMA formed								X	
IPMA	IPMA issues ICB									X

Figure 2-2. Predominant project management organizations.

If you live in:	Contact
Australia	AIPM
Great Britain	APM
Europe	IPMA
USA	PMI
USA	asapm
Elsewhere	IPMA

Because of the proliferation of PMI local chapters worldwide, you may decide to contact the PMI no matter what other organization is available.

Australian Institute for Project Management (AIPM)

The AIPM was formed in 1976 as the Project Managers' Forum and has been instrumental in progressing the profession of project management in Australia. The AIPM has over 3,000 members throughout Australia. The AIPM developed and documented their standards as the Australian National Competency Standards for Project Management (NCSPM). The AIPM uses the NCSPM as its basis for required knowledge and certification testing. The NCSPM provides for certification at six levels; these range from team member to multilevel program director. These levels are described in the Australian Qualification Framework (AQF). The AIPM currently certifies project managers only at three levels of the AQF. These levels are the middle to upper-middle levels of the AQF. The NCSPM incorporates the nine knowledge areas of the PMI's PMBOK directly into the knowledge part of their qualification program.

Certifications

Criteria: Australian National Competency Standards for Project Management (NCSPM)

Project Director/Program Manager (Level 6)
Project Manager (Level 5)
Project Team Member/Project Specialist (Level 4)

Contact Information

Australian Institute of Project Management (AIPM)
National Office
Level 9, 139

Macquarie St.
Sydney NSW 2000
Phone: 02 9252 7277
Fax: 02 9252 7077
E-mail: info@aipm.com.au
Web site: http://aipm.com.au/

How to Apply for Membership

Telephone. Call the headquarters using the telephone number above and tell them you are interested in joining. They will direct you to the proper office.

Online. Go to the AIPM Web site listed above. From the "Membership" pull-down menu, select "Application Forms," then select the proper form (most likely "Member"). This is a "pop-up." Follow the instructions.

Association for Project Management (APM)

The APM was formed about 1988 and adopted PRINCE as their standard. PRINCE stands for **PR**ojects **IN** **C**ontrolled **E**nvironments. PRINCE was derived from the standards developed for the Central Computer and Telecommunications Agency (CCTA). They later participated with the British government and other organizations in updating PRINCE to PRINCE2. PRINCE2 is maintained by the British government with input from the APM. The APM currently uses PRINCE2 as its basis for required knowledge and certification testing. PRINCE2 is a process-based approach with five stages for "enabling efficient control of resources and regular progress monitoring throughout the project."[1] The APM offers four levels of certification, from Associate Project Management Professional (Level 1) to Certificated International Project Manager (CIPM) (Level 4).

Certifications

Criteria: PRINCE2

Certificated International Project Manager (CIPM)
Senior Project Manager (Level 3)
Certified Project Manager (Level 2)
Associate Project Management Professional (Level 1)

Contact Information

Association for Project Management (APM)
50 West Wycombe Road
High Wycombe
Buckinghamshire

HP12 3AE
Phone: 01494 440090
Fax: 01494 528937
E-mail: services@apm.org.uk
Web site: http://www.apm.org.uk/

How to Apply for Membership

Telephone. Call the headquarters using the telephone number above and tell them you are interested in joining. They will direct you to the proper office.

Online. Go to the Web site listed above. Click on "Membership." Click on the appropriate membership level. Click on "Fees and How to Apply." Follow the instructions under "How to Apply."

American Society for the Advancement of Project Management (asapm)

The asapm was created in 2001. The stated mission of the asapm is "to provide opportunities for U.S. industry and individuals to improve their project management competencies. This is accomplished through a series of programs and projects that interchange information and demonstrate the "best practices" of the project management profession."[2] The asapm offers a broad array of competency assessments for different levels of stakeholders, with certifications for many of them.

The Levels

Senior management or project sponsor (SP)
Resource Managers (RM)
Project Office Manager (PO)
Project Directors or Program Managers of complex multi-organization projects (aCPM3)
Project Managers of large, complex projects (aCPM2)
Project Managers of medium or less-complex projects (aCPM1)
Project Team Members (TM)

Certifications for the asapm Certified Project Manager (aCPM) roles are currently under development. The asapm certifications incorporate the asapm National Competency Baseline, the Global Project Manager Performance-based Competency Standards and PMI's PMBOK as the knowledge base and requires that applicants for its certifications be current practitioners in the project management field. Their certification process assesses performance-based competency, rather than just knowledge, and follows the general guidelines of the IPMA (International Project Management Association) and requires extensive interviews by project management peers.

The asapm staff have cleverly incorporated the elements of their competency model into a software data set developed in the Microsoft Access format. They call this model "CompModel SixPack." A single-user copy is available on the Web site at: http://www.asapm.org/l_compmodel.asp.

The asapm always prints their acronym in lower case. When asked why, Stacy Goff said: ". . . We did it to reflect that our organization's purpose is to serve our members, so the lower case illustrates that subordinate status. We are here to serve our members, as opposed to the other way around. This is something that we feel is part of our differentiation, compared to some other organizations."[3]

Certifications

Criteria: IPMA's Competence Baseline, as adapted for the United States, plus the Global Project Manager Performance-Based Competency Standards

Project Directors or Program Managers of complex multi-organization projects (aCPM3)
Project Managers of large, complex projects (aCPM2)
Project Managers of medium or less-complex projects (aCPM1)

Contact Information

American Society for the Advancement of Project Management
P.O. Box 1945
Monument, CO 80132 USA
Phone: 931 647-7373
Fax: 931 647-7217
E-mail: info@asapm.org
Web site: http://asapm.org/

How to Apply for Membership

Telephone. Call the headquarters using the telephone number above and tell them you are interested in joining. They will direct you to the proper office.

Online. Go to the Web site and click on "Join asapm." Fill in the application and follow the instructions. Submit.

International Project Management Association (IPMA)

The IPMA was spawned by the APM and registered as an international organization in Switzerland in 1998. The IPMA created their International Project Management Base Competencies (IBC) in 1999 and uses them as the base for their certifications. The IPMA offers four levels of certification: Certificated Projects Director (Level A), Certificated Projects Manager (Level B), Certificated Project Management Professional (Level C), and Certificated Project Management Practitioner (Level D).

Certifications

Criteria: IPMA Competence Baseline (ICB)

Certificated Projects Director (Level A)
Certificated Projects Manager (Level B)
Certificated Project Management Professional (Level C)
Certificated Project Management Practitioner (Level D)

Contact Information

International Project Management Association
P.O. Box 1167, 3860 BD NIJKERK, The Netherlands
Tel: +31 33 247 34 30
Fax: +31 33 246 04 70
E-mail: info@ipma.ch
Web site: http://www.ipma.ch/

How to Apply for Membership

Note: Contact the IPMA through one of the means listed above and follow their instructions. You must join the IPMA through one of their associate members. The headquarters office will lead you through this process.

Telephone. Call the headquarters using the telephone number above and tell them you are interested in joining. They will direct you to the proper office.

Online. Go to the Web site listed above and click on info@ipma.ch. Send an e-mail message stating you wish to join the organization and request directions.

Project Management Institute (PMI)

The Project Management Institute was created in 1969 in New Castle, Pennsylvania.[4] The PMI was headquartered in Upper Darby, Pennsylvania, until 1999, when it moved to Newtown Square, Pennsylvania. The PMI is the foremost project management organization in the United States and has over 100,000 members throughout the world. The PMI released their first body of knowledge as the Project Management Body of Knowledge (PMBOK) in 1986. Subsequent updates were made to the BOK, and the last issuance was *A Guide to the Project Management Body of Knowledge (PMBOK) 2000*, issued in the year 2000, also referred to as *The PMBOK Guide*. The *PMBOK Guide* concentrates on the core attributes of an internal project and does a good job of that. The PMI uses the PMBOK as its basis for required knowledge and certification testing. The PMBOK lists nine areas that cover many subareas, which, if placed on an indentured list, would constitute about forty-six areas and subareas altogether. The PMI provides for certification at two levels: Project Management Professional (PMP) and Certified Associate Project Manager (CAPM). A third level, consisting of numerous subdivisions, was temporarily introduced to "tailor" qualification requirements to specific industries, but this is presently being held in abeyance.

Certifications

Criteria: Project Management Knowledge areas (in PMBOK)

Project Management Professional (PMP)
Certified Associate in Project Management (CAPM)

Contact Information

Project Management Institute (PMI)
Four Campus Boulevard
Newtown Square, PA 19073-3299 USA
Phone: 610 356-4600
Fax: 610 356-4647
E-mail: pmihq@pmi.org
Web site: http://www.pmi.org

How to Apply for Membership

Telephone. Call the headquarters using the telephone number above and tell them you are interested in joining. They will direct you to the proper office.

Online. Go to the PMI Web site shown above. Under "Membership," "Become a Member." Click on "Apply for Membership" and follow the instructions.

American Management Association (AMA)

The AMA was founded in 1926 as a nonprofit organization. It is the preeminent management association of America and offers seminars, conferences, and forums and briefings on current issues. Through its publications arm, AMACOM, the AMA offers books and publications, and print and online self-study courses. The AMA offers many certificates for attending their training courses and seminars but does not provide certification, *per se*, for project managers.

Contact Information

American Management Association (AMA)
1601 Broadway New York, NY 10019
Customer Service
Phone: 800 262-9699
Fax: 518 891-0368
E-mail: customerservice@amanet.org
Web site: http://www.amanet.org/

How to Apply for Membership

Telephone. Call customer service using the telephone number above and tell them you are interested in joining. They will direct you to the proper office.

Online. Go to: http://www.amanet.org/joinama/index.htm. Select one of the subsets of either "Companies" or "Individual" and follow instructions.

Standards Organizations

Many of the above organizations desire that their standards be accepted at a higher level. In order to accomplish this, the developing organization submits its standard to the higher-level authority for consideration. The considering authority usually takes some time to evaluate the standard, comparing it to others in the same field and making recommendations for changes, if necessary. Depending on the acceptance of the changes by the developing organization, the standard is accepted or rejected by the considering authority. Presently, several project management organizations have submitted their body of knowledge to higher authorities to be sanctioned by that authority. At the present time, the American National Standards Institute (ANSI) has accepted the PMBOK as a standard. The National Standards Systems Network (NSSN), American Society for Quality Control (ASQC), and International Organization for Standardization (ISO) are considering that same move. Understandably, the IPMA has submitted its body of knowledge and standards to the ISO for consideration as well. Figure 2-3 shows a summary of these activities.

Technical Standards Organizations

In addition to the project management standards, you will encounter the standards of many organizations that will affect the technical aspects of your project. The American National Standards Institute (ANSI), the American Society for Quality Control (ASQC), the Interna-

Figure 2-3. National and international organizations authorizing standards.

Standard/Body of Knowledge	Developer	Considering Body
PMBOK	PMI	ANSI
PMBOK	PMI	NSSN
PMBOK	PMI	ISO
PMBOK	PMI	ASQC
IPMA Competence Baseline	IPMA	ISO
National Competency Standards for Project Management	AIPM	None known
PRINCE2	APM	None known

tional Standards Organization (ISO), the Institute of Electrical and Electronic Engineers (IEEE), and the Software Engineering Institute (SEI), just to name a few. I have to limit it to a few because the last time I counted, I found over 150 such organizations, and I probably missed several at that. These few will give you an idea of the scope, content, and breadth of the bodies and their standards.

These kinds of standards are usually referenced in the "Reference Documents" section of your Requirements Document. As I said, these standards can affect the technical aspects of your project, and it is your responsibility to ensure these standards (at least the parts that are referenced) are available to your technical people in the performance of their tasks.

Notes

1. *Managing Successful Projects with PRINCE2* (London: The Stationary Office, 2002).
2. http://www.asapm.org/a_mission.asp.
3. Part of the text of an e-mail from Stacy Goff, PMP, asapm VP, Webmaster, and Education Director to the author on 20 October 2003.
4. http://www.pmi.org/info/AP_IntroOverview.asp?nav=0201.

CHAPTER 3

Considering the Project Management Organizations

In Chapter 2, the principal organizations were introduced. There we found that the organizations are essentially geographically oriented. Now, in order to accommodate where you are in your career, we need to enter another variable. That variable is the basis for certification. You will see that there are two bases for certification. You can use these variables in selecting the "right" organization for you both geographically and from the basis of certification.

The Current State of the Art

While the art of project management is still emerging, it is reasonably stable in its core content—that is, the content concerning what to do once a project is initiated.

There are two trains of thought as to what a project manager is or should be. To see these two ideas, we'll look at the certification processes. The certification processes fall into two groups: "Knowledge-Based" and "Competency-Based." The PMI is the primary user of the "Knowledge-Based" approach; AIPM, APM, asapm, and IPMA use the "Competency-Based" approach. The PMI certifies at two levels; the others certify at three to five levels.

In terms of size, however, the PMI is head and shoulders above all the rest. The PMI touts over 100,000 members worldwide; the IPMA has 30,000 members; the APM has 13,000 members; and the AIPM has about 3,700 members. The asapm is just emerging, and no membership figures are yet available.

Where Is Project Management Going from Here?

As technology has opened new vistas we couldn't even dream of even ten years ago, I believe that project management is going broader and higher and more virtual. This means that project management and its standards and organizations are still evolving.

By broader, I mean more encompassing. For instance, if you compare the PMBOK to the APMBOK to the P2M to PRINCE2 to the ICB, you will find significant differences. The fundamental differences in the certification process is that the PMI is knowledge-based and the others are competency-based. It appears that each organization has generated its certifications based on its own ideas of what project management is or should be and what market they want to serve. In order to grow, it also appears to me that any organization would want to be as broad and all-encompassing as it can be. That's why I think it's going to be broader.

By higher, I mean more international. Right now, the most serious competitors for international "conquest" are the PMI and the IPMA. Each organization serves many, many countries, and in many cases there are overlaps. That means that if you live in Austria, Finland, France, Germany, Greece, Italy, Portugal, or dozens of other countries, you actually can select the organization you belong to.

The PMI is a centralized organization with radials extending to the various countries. The elements in the various countries are simply components of the PMI. The IPMA, on the other hand, is a confederation of organizations that subscribe to its standards. It is decentralized. Will the two merge? I doubt it. The concepts of each are quite different, and it would take a lot of doing to get them together. However, both PMI and IPMA have submitted their bodies of knowledge and their certification processes to higher (that is, international) organizations such as ISO. Clearly, both organizations want to be thought of as "higher."

By more virtual, I mean that many more projects will take advantage of the "virtual" phenomenon and move in that direction. The World Wide Web as a communication and data vehicle opened the floodgates. Every day more and more projects and programs are being conducted remotely than ever before. We refer to this phenomenon as "Virtual Projects."[1] Typically, a virtual project has team members in various, different locations. Sometimes they are in different locations on campus, and sometimes in different states or countries. The combinations are limitless. Conducting a virtual project is similar to conducting a traditional project, but it requires extensive communication and control that traditional projects do not. The gains in productivity and decreased cost are achieved at the risk of monumental failure unless the project manager keeps the virtual project on the straight and narrow. Nevertheless, virtual projects are the wave of the future. Virtual projects will be discussed in more depth in Chapter 9.

There are some potentially exciting changes in the hopper right now. As of this writing, the ideas are just beginning to gel, but soon they will be developed and could change the mainstream ideas of the project management bodies of knowledge and the project management processes. These ideas are loosely grouped into the general category of "Knowledge Management" (KM). The idea is that KM is dynamic and vertically integrated, while the standard bodies of knowledge and practices are static and horizontally integrated. The bodies of knowledge (BOKs) determine or follow the flow of work, while KM follows knowledge generated in the process.

And now my personal opinion: I would like to see a melding of the breadth of the NCSPM with the "hard-core-what-to-do" approach of the PMBOK into an all-encompassing standard that includes the enterprise with the project and elevates them both to serve international needs. The IPMA approach of having a core set of areas and then allowing "electives" to be taught to compensate for differences in culture, approach, and so on, is a brilliant idea. Perhaps the asapm working with the IPMA can become the catalyst for this action. Add to this the concept of virtual projects and make allowances for KM, and there is no end where the knowledge base of project management can go.

Selecting the "Right" Organization for You

This issue begs two questions: Where are you in your career? and Where, geographically, do you or will you practice?

Where are you in your career? If you are just beginning your project management career, and by that I mean in school or in the first three years of practice, then the "right" answer is the PMI. The PMI PMBOK establishes the knowledge base for practically all the other organizations. The exception is the APM. Even at that, the PMI PMBOK is still just as useful in these organizations because the BOK is essentially universal. After the first three years, you may want to consider adding one of the other organizations based on where you practice. Why do I say "after three years?" Because the certification processes of the other organizations require and test experience in project management. Even though the PMI requires experience, their certification process does not test it. Whether you are early or later in your career, the American

Management Association (AMA) is always a good bet to provide continuing educational books, courses, and seminars in project management and general management as well.

Where, geographically, do you practice? The answer to this question may have an impact on which organization you choose. For instance, if you practice in Australia, you will likely want to belong to the Australian Institute of Project Management (AIPM). If you practice in Great Britain, you will likely want to belong to the Association of Project Management (APM). If you practice in Japan, you will likely want to belong to the (JPMF). All these organizations are geographically oriented. Next comes a compound situation. Once you have become established in your career, if you practice in the United States, you will likely want to belong to the Association for the Advancement of Project Management (asapm). If you practice internationally, you will likely want to belong to the International Project Management Association (IPMA) through a local chapter.

If you belong to one of the geographically oriented organizations, should you cancel your membership in the PMI or AMA? My answer is an emphatic: No! Both these organizations have offerings that are of great value to you no matter where you practice. The same statement holds true no matter where you are in your career.

Now, let's look at the language of project management.

Note

1. *Virtual* in this document refers to the *programmatic virtual*—that is, parts of the project are remotely located. These elements of the project organization are usually connected electronically (through the World Wide Web and other communication links). This is distinct from a *technical virtual* project, where the object of a game is simulated and represented virtually. A military training scenario, where soldiers shoot at video screens with laser gun attachments, is an example of a *technical virtual* project.

CHAPTER 4

Speaking the Language

If one thing is certain in project management right now, it is that the terminology varies from organization to organization and from company to company. So that we have a common vocabulary, I will explain the terms I use. Some of these terms are the same ones used by various organizations and some are different. Today, it can be difficult to "talk the talk" without a common vocabulary.

Based on my experience and research in project and program management, I have found that the field of projects and programs can be divided into seven categories:

- Small Project
- Intermediate Project
- Large Project
- Program
- Virtual Project or Program
- International Project or Program
- Large-Scale Project or Program

In order to manage these seven categories of projects or programs, I have found five levels of skill sets are required. The five skill sets are:

- Basic
- Advanced
- Expert
- Specialist
- Principal

It may be possible to define seven skill sets to match the seven categories, except that the discriminators between the intermediate and large projects are principally those of size and therefore simply require more of the same. The discriminators between specialty projects or programs, however, is a totally different matter. The specialty category is a summary of every unique category of project or program that can or does exist. The Specialist Skill Set is the corresponding skill set required to lead each of the unique categories. In other words, the breadth and depth of the specialty category and Specialist Skill Set are indeterminable but internally related.

The international type is really a specialty. However, it is so unique in its requirements that I have chosen to call it a separate group.

The span of control that a leader is allowed is equally broad. I find that there are five leadership roles in the field of project and program management. These roles are:

- Coordinator
- Supervisor
- Manager
- Director
- Vice President

Interestingly, it is not the responsibility that differentiates the roles. Rather, it is the authority of each role that makes the difference.

In Chapter 4, we will examine the characteristics of the categories, the skill sets, and the roles. I will cross-reference all of them using tables and explanations.

I explained some of the differences in the terminology used for phases, processes, and stages in Part I. Now, I will explain projects and programs, skills and leadership roles, and compare the program categories to the other factors.

Project and Program Types

As I said at the outset, project management terminology varies from organization to organization and from company to company. There is some standardization, but there is a lot of variability as well. If you were to invite all of those who have contributed to the current lexicon into one room and go through the terms that have already been defined, I'm sure you would get good arguments as to why each term is defined the way it is. I'm sure each has good reasons for being different. I am of the opinion that these terms do not need mathematical precision so long as you and I understand what we are talking about when we are talking.

Earlier, I introduced seven types of projects and programs. These types are distinguished by size, organization, complexity, and risk level.

Many project management organizations use different terminology. By their terminology, essentially everything is a project. A program, by their definition, is a group of projects. I disagree with this definition because a giant leap must be made in the skill set requirements between leading a project and leading a program. A project, by my definition, is accomplished for a customer inside an organization and a program is accomplished for a customer outside the company under a contract.

A Small Project

A small project is led by a project coordinator. It usually involves less than six people, who are of the same or closely related disciplines. A small project is a simple task of low complexity and low risk.

An Intermediate Project

An intermediate project is led by a project coordinator or a project supervisor. It generally involves six or more people, and the individuals are usually of different disciplines. An intermediate project is a task of moderate complexity and low to moderate risk.

A Large Project

A large project is led by a project manager. It generally consists of more than ten people, and the individuals are of different disciplines. A large project is a task of moderate to high complexity and moderate to high risk.

A Program

A program is led by a program manager. It is distinguished from a project by the existence of a legal contract between the company and the customer. A program generally consists of more than ten people, who are of different disciplines. A program is a task of moderate to high complexity and moderate to high risk.

A Virtual Project or Program

A virtual project or program is led by a project manager or a program manager. It is distinguished from other projects by the fact that two or more of the principal contributors (i.e., not vendors) are located in different geographical areas and interface only by means other than face-to-face (i.e., electronically). A virtual project or program generally consists of more than ten people who are of different disciplines. A virtual project or program is a task of moderate to high complexity and moderate to high risk.

An International Program

An international program is led by a program manager. It is distinguished from other programs by the fact that the customer is in a country other than the one managing the program.

There are some variations on this theme however, brought about by how multinational companies do business. Although you would expect an international program to be a program, it may be a project in a multinational company. In this instance, the product is manufactured in the home country and delivered to a branch office (sometimes registered as a different company) in the foreign country. The product is then handed over from the branch office to the customer.

Why this strange twist? This is because only the branch office, not the home office, is chartered to do business in that country. It is brought about by the customer's need to have a local entity to hold legally responsible.

An international program generally consists of more than ten people of different disciplines. An international program is a task of moderate to high complexity and moderate to high risk. Complexity and risk usually refer more to programmatic issues than to technical issues.

A Large-Scale Program

A large-scale program is led by a program manager, a program director, or a program vice president. It is distinguished from other programs by the size and organization of the program—that is, a large-scale program is divided into smaller projects. A large-scale program generally consists of more than fifty people of different disciplines. It involves a task of moderate to high complexity and moderate to high risk. Complexity and risk apply to programmatic issues and technical issues.

Characterizing a project or program lays the groundwork for defining the skills necessary for a project manager to lead it.

Project and Program Skill Sets

I see the need for five skill sets to accomplish the project leadership tasks of today's projects. While I agree with Jim Lewis[1] in thinking that a single person is not a project and that project managers should not have technical tasks to accomplish in addition to their project tasks, I would be amiss if I did not recognize that this is the way a lot of so-called projects are assigned and conducted in industry today. Even though I don't agree with this approach, it is a fact of life, and I have included it in the skill sets I have defined.

The skill sets are:

- Basic Skill Set
- Advanced Skill Set
- Expert Skill Set
- Specialty Skill Set
- Principal Skill Set

Basic Skill Set

The Basic Skill Set requires an understanding of the technical task to be performed and the purpose and content of the project. In fact, all skill sets require this understanding. The Basic Skill Set includes the most basic skills required to conduct a project. These skills are an appreciation of what projects are all about and an understanding and ability to manage the content of a project, to create and maintain a schedule for the project, and to create and account for a budget for the project.

Advanced Skill Set

The Advanced Skill Set includes all the subjects of the Basic Skill Set at an advanced level. Additionally, many other subjects are added to create an understanding of an organization and the skills necessary for people to operate in an organization. The Advanced Skill Set requires an appreciation for risk and complexity. Other skills, such as configuration control and change management, now enter the picture, as does the ability to divide the task into workable units and to establish and track values for those units.

Expert Skill Set

The Expert Skill Set includes all the subjects of the previous skill sets and adds sales, teaming and partnering, proposals, negotiating, business considerations, legal considerations, sophisticated estimating, and more complex metrics for tracking program status. The expert level is more sensitive to management's need for profit and to customer needs in general.

Specialty Skill Set

The Specialty Skill Set contains all the previous skill sets and adds unique and special knowledge for specialized situations. These programs include international programs where specialized knowledge of the customer's habits, laws, and customs are a necessity. The Specialty Skill Set is distinguished by its uniqueness, no matter what it is. Special knowledge is also needed to conduct a virtual program. These are programs where major contributors are located at places that can only be reached electronically, places where there can be no face-to-face contact with the participants.

Principal Skill Set

The Principal Skill Set contains the subjects of all the previous skill sets at a superior level. The manager competent in the Principal Skill Set is expected to know all the "Firm" and "Soft" subjects that apply to project and program management and will specialize in general management. This manager will delegate much of the "Firm" day-to-day activity, such as accounting and scheduling, and spend his or her time in solving problems, expanding the position of the company (selling), and understanding the wants as well as the specific needs of the customer.

Figure 4-1 help you visualize how skill sets apply to project and program categories.

Leadership Roles

Here, I am defining five leadership roles for project and program management. These roles are:

- Project Coordinator
- Project Supervisor

Figure 4-1. Skill sets as they apply to project and program categories.

Skill Set	Project/Program Category
Basic	Small Project
Advanced	Intermediate Project Large Project
Expert	Program
Specialty	Virtual Project or Program International Program
Principal	Large-Scale Program

- Project or Program Manager
- Program or Programs Director
- Program or Programs Vice President

One can argue that two other roles exist, these being project engineer and project lead. However, I consider these as primarily technical roles, and despite their leadership responsibility, not really part of project management. I will stick to my five roles.

Today, industry has begun calling every project leader a project manager when, as you will see, several of these leaders are not managers at all. Nevertheless, management has delegated to them the responsibility of leading a project even without much authority.

Coordinator

A project coordinator is responsible for ensuring that all the established contributing elements supporting a task are available at the right time and in the right order to accomplish the task.

Supervisor

A project supervisor is responsible for the conduct and completion of the project under his or her supervision. A project supervisor has the ability and authority to move resources within the project to ensure that the project meets its task, schedule, quality, and budget requirements.

Manager

A project manager is responsible for achieving project objectives, customer satisfaction, and project completion. A program manager is responsible for achieving a program's profit objectives and customer satisfaction, and may be responsible for growth of the value of the program. Project and program managers have the ability and authority to move resources into, within, and out of a project or program to ensure that it meets its task, schedule, quality, and budget requirements. A program manager has profit and loss responsibility.

Director

A program director is responsible for achieving profit objectives, customer satisfaction, and growth of the value of the sum of the programs under his or her jurisdiction. A program director has the ability and authority to change program resources and to direct program managers to make changes necessary to achieve overall program needs. Two titles frequently exist within this category: program director and programs director. A program director directs a large or very large program; a programs director directs a group of related programs.

Vice President

A program vice president is responsible for achieving the profit objectives, customer satisfaction, and growth of the value of the sum of the programs under his or her jurisdiction. A program vice president has the ability and authority to determine which program and projects will be pursued and bid, and the ability and authority to establish priorities for the utilization of resources within programs. Again, two titles may exist within this category: program vice president and programs vice president. A program vice president directs a huge program; a programs vice president directs a group of programs.

Figure 4-2 will help you to visualize how roles apply to project and program categories.

Now, let's go on to Part II, where the skill sets will be expanded to show the subject areas contained and how they are applied to projects and programs of varying sizes and types.

Figure 4-2. Leadership roles as they apply to project and program categories.

Role	Project/Program Category
Coordinator	Small Project Intermediate Project
Supervisor	Intermediate Project
Manager	Large Project Program
Director	Program Large-Scale Program
Vice President	Large-Scale Program

Note

1. James Lewis, *Fundamentals of Project Management* (New York: AMACOM Books, 2001).

PART

II

ACQUIRING PROJECT MANAGEMENT SKILLS

This part of the book is dedicated to presenting the primary project management skill sets you need in order to lead the several levels of projects that exist. It is assumed you already have the technical skills to either perform the technical task or appreciate and understand all the disciplines necessary to accomplish the technical task.

As stated in the preface, the first element of the success formula is knowledge. Knowledge is achieved in a three-step process: awareness, training, and education. Awareness is: What you need to do. Training is: How to do it. Education is: Why you need to do it.

This part of the book will create the awareness of the subject areas you need in order to perform at the various levels of project and program management. Once awareness is achieved, I direct you to the training that will support the early levels of the skill set needs. Chapter 7 in Part III will introduce expanded training and education in all these areas.

Part II is presented in two chapters. Chapter 5 addresses acquiring preparatory skills—that is, those skills every project manager needs at every level of performance. Preparatory skills are divided into two groups: Personal Skills and Company/Customer/Industry Skills. Chapter 6 addresses the subject area needs of the five skill groups that comprise the project and program management fields. Reading through this part of the book, you may ask: Who has time to read all these books or to attend all these seminars? My answer is that you need to make time. On long coast-to-coast flights or while waiting for your plane to load are good opportunities for reading. A boring evening in the hotel room is another good opportunity. Reading at lunch has a double return—you can gain some knowledge and lose some weight at the same time. Personally, I have two stacks of books that I call the "Takers" and the "Leavers." Size dictates which pile a book ends up in. The "Takers" I take on trips. Reading time is pretty much up to you, so you need to work it into your schedule. Seminars are pretty much up to the company. You need to take the seminars offered as standard fare by the company and then expand your horizons by requesting to attend the applicable ones recommended by this book or others you come across in your own research.

CHAPTER 5

Acquiring Preparatory Skills

Before we jump into the specific subjects necessary to prepare you for each type of project or program, we need to discuss some preparatory skills you must have. These skills fall into two groups: the Personal Skill Set and the Company/Industry Skill Set.

Personal Skill Set

The Personal Skill Set are those skills every project and program manager needs in order to lead their tasks and teams effectively. These include problem solving, leadership, ethics, and presentation skills. Each of these skills has an infinite number of competence levels that can be achieved. To one degree or another, you already possess some of these skills, and you will continue to refine them throughout your career.

Problem Solving

Problem solving is fundamental to project management. It is the most important of the personal skills. The mechanics of problem solving are essentially the same, no matter what. They involve defining the problem, searching for alternative solutions, evaluating them, selecting the best alternative solution, and then applying it. There are some sophisticated software applications that present these mechanics, but they all use about the same process.

Applying the achieved solutions will contribute to your knowledge base. Should you confront the same kinds of issues over time, you will gain a knowledge base of solutions applicable to these issues. At that point, of course, you will only need to apply the solution rather than start from the beginning every time. Most importantly, though, you will be able to anticipate these problems and build solutions into the project plan before the problem actually exhibits itself. Nevertheless, other problems will crop up, and you will need to apply the process again and again.

Leadership

In my opinion, John Maxwell defined leadership precisely when he wrote: "Leadership is influence, nothing more, nothing less."[1] When prosecuting a project, you will find the need for leadership everywhere, every day. But leadership is not something you can pour out of a bottle, nor is it a mathematical formula. It is an elusive trait that some people are born with, some people develop, some people don't have, and some never will. Whatever it is, Ken Blanchard is right: A "pill" just won't work.[2] Remember the "persona" factor I talked about earlier? Your abilities as a leader will be greatly influenced by your persona.

You can get a leg up on the development of your leadership skills and style through courses (seminars), such as *Preparing for Leadership: What It Takes to Take the Lead* offered by the American Management Association (AMA). They say, "This course is uniquely designed to help leaders-to-be get ready for their new challenges and responsibilities."[3]

Ethics

Webster defines ethics as: "The principles of conduct governing an individual or group." As a project manager, your ethics will be tested with every decision you make, so it is important to have an understanding not only of ethics in a general sense but of the ethics that are the governing principles for your industry, your company, and your discipline. These can sometimes clash, and that is where your individual ethics are tested. How you pass this test is a reflection of your integrity.

Samuel Southard's *Ethics for Executives* offers the traditional view of business ethics, while John Maxwell's *There's No Such Thing As "Business" Ethics: There's Only One Rule for Making Decisions* offers a different and interesting view. Many times ethics will be severely tested when dealing with international programs. Here is where culture plays an important role.

Most universities have an ethics department that handles ethical issues for the business-associated curricula as well as for the entire college or university. These offices are good sources for information on ethics. If you happen to be involved with government contracts in the defense sector, the Defense Industry Initiative (DII)[4] is a good source for information.

Most of the principal organizations have an ethics requirement; meaning you must accept their ethics standards (frequently called a Code of Conduct), in order to be certified by them. You can find the standards in Figure 5-1.

Meeting and Presentation Skill Set

Refined meeting and presentation skills are essential for all project managers. For discussion purposes I consider public speaking and visual aids as inherent parts of presentation skills.

Your meeting skills will be tested every time you call a meeting, formal or informal. All meetings need to be called for a purpose and managed to that purpose. The purpose of the meeting should be stated on the agenda if it is a formal meeting.

A trick that has always worked for me is to open the meeting with a salutation (good morning) and then say: "The purpose of this meeting, is . . ." and then, of course, state the purpose of the meeting. This lets the attendees know there is a purpose and a structure to the meeting, and it's not just to get together for coffee and donuts. Nor is it for airing all the grievances in the world.

Your presentation skills will be tested every time you stand up for a meeting, for a monthly review or a customer review, or at any other time you are the center of attention—and as a project manager, you will almost always be the center of attention. Although there are a lot of books that address the subject of public speaking and presentations, most are mechanical in their presentation. However, I have found a

Figure 5-1. Organizational ethics references.

Organization	Reference(s)
APM (Code of Conduct)	Association for Project Management, *By-Laws*, association for Project Management, Buckinghamshire, UK, 2002.
asapm	http://www.asapm.org/a_ethics.asp
PMI (Code of Professional Conduct)	Code of conduct: http://www.pmi.org/prod/groups/public/documents/info/PDC_PMPCodeOfConductFil e.asp Part of: Project Management Institute, *Project Management Professional Certification Handbook* (Newton Square, PA: Project Management Institute, 2000): 22. [PMP Handbook]

little book by Steve Mandel titled *Effective Presentation Skills* that is good for individual study. This book has a lot of checklists and self-assessments to help you with the basic skills. This is most certainly a skill, though, that can only be mastered with practice. Practice worked for Demosthenes, and it will work for you. Once again, your persona will have a great deal to do with how you project your speaking abilities.

If your company doesn't offer a course in public speaking or presentation skills, you can check with your local community college or simply join Toastmasters International.[5] I firmly believe that presentation skills must be refined and reinforced in a group environment.

In the workaday world, presentation skills are closely allied to the visual aids you will use in your presentations. The visual aids can vary from handouts to flip charts to overhead viewgraphs to 35-millimeter slides to television presentations. The tools can vary from a typewriter to a computer using the ubiquitous Microsoft Power Point to sophisticated video software. The key to presentation skills lies in maintaining an audience's interest and conveying the necessary information to them. Make certain your media supports and enhances your presentation data and is not just a crutch for a bad presentation, as in the cartoon where the salesman stands up and says: "I don't have anything to say but I do have some neat slides."

It is possible that your company prefers to use one particular presentation technique. Needless to say, that's the technique you should concentrate on. The training department should select the presentation skills seminar for your company; this way, the consistency of presentations will be ensured throughout the company. If you don't have a training department and there are no standards in your company, my opinion is that Microsoft Power Point is the most universal tool you can use to create your presentation media. The resulting presentation can be printed for handouts, converted into overhead slides (view graphs) or 35-millimeter slides, be presented as direct video, or used to drive video projection equipment. The Help menu that is a part of the application will even establish formats for you.

If you are a veteran project manager, the above paragraphs will likely be the things you do as a matter of course. But, if you're just starting out, I suggest you pay close attention to those paragraphs. Develop these skills before you need them. It's a demeaning experience to stand in front of an audience and get chewed out for presenting a "bunch of unintelligible gobbledygook," or to be taken to task by your boss for having poor decision-making skills, or to be chastised by your team members for not providing adequate leadership, but to me, the worst thing of all is to be accused of not having ethics! These skills are fundamental to your growth and position as a project manager. Learn them and use them well.

Company/Customer/Industry Skill Set

The Company/Customer/Industry Skill Set consists of three groups of documentation. The first group is that used by your company to convey the policies, plans, processes, and procedures established by management to control the business of the company. The second group is the documentation used by the customers with whom the company does business. This documentation sets standards and requirements for both the customer and the customer's suppliers. Federal Acquisition Regulations (FARs) and NASA Procurement Regulations (NASA PRs) are typical of documentation in this group. The third group is the documentation of organizations created to establish standards, processes, and procedures for specific equipment or industries. The Software Engineering Institute (SEI), the Underwriter's Laboratory (UL), and the International Standards Organization (ISO) are typical of organizations in this group.

Enterprise Policies, Plans, and Procedures

This is the simplest of all the skills. All you need to do is to read, understand, and remember the policies, plans, processes, and procedures established by your company. If you are working for a company, you must understand how that company does business. Now that may seem like an obvious recommendation, but it is amazing the number of people, especially those who "know it all," who don't take the time to read the policy manuals of their company. This can really get you into trouble, especially when you are composing your project plan. Usually, company policies are referred to as the "Red Book," or the "Blue Book," or the "Granite Book" or some similar term to bring attention to the importance of the book. Whatever its name, it usually has a venerated place in the minds of management and should be treated accordingly.

The best way to start this process is to list all the documents and then find them. Usually, these documents are divided into sections for Administration, Human Resources, Engineering, Program Management, and so on. Make a list of the documents that are applicable to you and to projects and get on with reading them.

Figure 5-2 shows the typical categories of documentation you will find in company policies, plans, processes, and procedures.

Company policies, plans, and procedures can usually be grouped into two classes: too few or too many. The numbers of policies in a company are usually directly proportional to the number of employees in a company. Small companies have few policies; very large companies have many, many policies. This is understandable, but unfortunately, there is a "critical mass" of categories of policies and procedures that every company should have, and the small companies usually do not cover all these categories. It is important to understand this principle if you are a part of a small company. The lack of policies and procedures can allow for a lot of latitude, but this can also get you into trouble. If

Figure 5-2. Typical company documentation categories.

Number	Category
1000	Customer
2000	Administration
3000	Finance
4000	Legal & Contracts
5000	Personnel/Human Resources
6000	Materiel
7000	Planning
8000	Research & Development
9000	Quality
10000	Business Development
11000	Programs
12000	Engineering
13000	Manufacturing & Production
14000	Field Operations
15000	Operations & Maintenance

you are part of a small company with very few policies and procedures, cultivate an understanding with management about their expectations. Your job is to figure out what policies your company has, where they are, and which apply to you and to which projects. Read these policies (when available) and understand them. Why? Because this step is fundamental to the creation of a project plan within the context of how your company operates.

Customer Standards

If you are leading a project that performs tasks within your own organization, it is likely that group will use the same policies and procedures as your group does. If you are leading a project that performs tasks within your own corporation or consortium but with another company, it is likely that company will have policies and procedures different from your own. If you are leading a program that performs a task under contract, customer standards are the documents of the customers that apply to you as a contractor or vendor. These standards and regulations may have to do with procurement or with task performance. Required customer standards should be listed in the statement of work, but may not be. Take some time to review prior statements of work and talk with the customer to ferret out any customer standards that may be required but were not listed. Why? Because when handover time comes, the customer may say: "We expected you to know these standards were required. That's partly why we hired you." There's little you can say to win this argument.

Industry Standards and Regulations

Standards and regulations refer to the documents that govern the products and processes your project will create. Bodies such as the American Society for Quality Control (ASQC), the International Standards Organization (ISO), the Institute of Electrical and Electronic Engineers (IEEE), and so on have been created specifically for the purpose of establishing and maintaining specific standards and regulations.

How does this affect you? If your product is software, it's a pretty sure bet you will use the standards of the Software Engineering Institute (SEI). If your project is involved with electrical products, most certainly the standards and requirements of the Underwriter's Laboratory (UL) will be involved. If your project is involved with mechanical products, the requirements of the American National Standards Institute (ANSI) will be involved, and so on. The required standards and regulations should be included in your statement of work or your specification but may be glossed over there. If you are new to the product, take some time to review past specifications and talk with the technical people who have been involved with these products in the past. It will be worth your time.

There are over 150 bodies setting standards for everything from airports to pharmaceuticals to toilets. As project manager, you may or may not need to know each of these standards and regulations by chapter and verse, but you must know which are required and how to ensure that copies are available to the technical people on the project. Failure to adhere to these standards and regulations can cause the product to be unresponsive and can cause the project to fail.

Because each company and each project is different, knowledge of the foregoing skills will be an individualized affair. Nevertheless, at least now you have an idea of what they are and where to look for them.

Suggested Reading (Books)

Blanchard, Ken. *The Leadership Pill*. New York: Free Press, 2003.

Mandel, Steve. *Effective Presentation Skills*. Menlo Park, Calif.: Crisp Pubs, 1993.

Maxwell, John C. *The 21 Irrefutable Laws of Leadership*. Nashville, Tenn.: Thomas Nelson Publishers, 1998.

Maxwell, John. *There's No Such Thing as "Business" Ethics: There's Only One Rule for Making Decisions*. New York: Warner Books, 2003.

Southard, Samuel. *Ethics for Executives*. Nashville, Tenn.: T. Nelson, 1975.

Seminar Contacts

Preparing for Leadership: What It Takes to Take the Lead
See: http://www.amanet.org/seminars/cmd2/2536.htm

Notes

1. John C. Maxwell, *The 21 Irrefutable Laws of Leadership*, (Nashville, Tenn.: Thomas Nelson Publishers, 1998).
2. Ken Blanchard, *The Leadership Pill* (New York: Free Press, 2003).
3. *Preparing for Leadership: What It Takes to Take the Lead* (New York: AMA), see: http://www.amanet.org/seminars/cmd2/2536.htm.
4. For further information about the Defense Industry Initiative, contact: Richard J. Bednar, Senior Counsel, Crowell & Moring LLP, 1001 Pennsylvania Avenue, N.W., Suite 1000, Washington, D.C. 20004-2595, Telephone: 202-624-2619; e-mail: rbednar@crowell.com.
5. http://www.toastmasters.org/.

CHAPTER 6

Acquiring Project and Program Skills

Based on my experience and research in the field of project and program management, I have found there are at least forty-seven subject areas required to address the needs of projects and programs. I group these forty-seven subject areas into five skill sets. Why five skill sets? Because they coincide with what I know to be the general requirements for the various levels of projects and programs that one is likely to encounter. I have chosen the terms: Basic, Advanced, Expert, Specialty, and Principal to classify the levels.

As you read through the skill sets, you will see that the first line of each group defines what separates that level from the previous one. The skill sets coincide, to a degree, with those of the major organizations. But each organization has categorized these skills into different levels or groups for its own reasons. None is wrong. It's just that each has a different reason for creating different skill sets. The point of it all, though, is that it takes essentially the same skills to conduct a project or program no matter how you group the skills.

The skill sets presented here are *not* for the purpose of preparing you for some certification test in one of the organizations. For that, you need to follow the guidelines of the organization, precisely. My purpose is to establish the skill sets to be consistent with the requirements of the types of projects and programs you are likely to encounter in the real world.

As you read through the following skill sets you will find an introduction and a description together with a level of experience and the proficiency required for each level. The introduction presents the discriminators that separate the current level from the previous level. The description provides the scope of activity involved with a position. The experience stipulates the experience necessary at the *prior level* to achieve entry to the current level. Proficiency shows the subjects that must be mastered, and at what level, in order to be proficient at the level under discussion.

The project- and program-level requirements are cumulative. Before attaining the Expert Level, a manager must have completed all the requirements for the Basic Level and the Advanced Level.

In each of the following skill set descriptions you will see a table labeled Basic Skill Set, Advanced Skill Set, and so on. The columns in these tables have the following meanings:

The far left column contains a number. That number is simply a reference number for the subject. Next is the subject title. Following that is a column containing a single letter: F, S, or C. These letters stand for firm, soft, or combination, and refer to the skill type of the subject. A firm task is one that is objective by nature and remains constant; it is not subject to interpretation. Some refer to the firm task as a "hard" task. I have chosen to call it firm to differentiate it from a "difficult" task. A soft task is one that uses some interpretation in its application. The "Skill Type" column is followed by the abbreviated definition of the subject. The definition is followed by three columns labeled: PMI, APM, and ICB, respectively. These columns show a reference to a PMI PMBOK paragraph that further defines the subject or the APM BOK that further defines the subject or the ICB element that further defines the subject.

Following each skill set table is a second table that relates each subject in that skill set to the proficiency level necessary for that subject. The top number refers to the reference number, and the bottom number refers to the proficiency required, using the following taxonomy:

1. The individual must be able to apply the Basic Skill Set and have a proficiency of the remaining subjects as indicated.
2. The individual must have a thorough understanding of the subjects indicated and be able to apply advanced knowledge, backed by appropriate experience, to the projects he or she is leading.
3. The individual must have an understanding of the subject area indicated and be able to apply expert knowledge, backed by appropriate experience, to the projects he or she is leading.

4. The individual must have an understanding of the subject area indicated and be able to apply advanced or expert knowledge, backed by appropriate experience, to the projects he or she is leading.
5. The individual at this level must be expert in all subjects. Many of the details of the subjects will be delegated to subordinates but this individual must approve the subject delegation and the resulting product.

Some subjects will mature or "top out" at some level and show that level for all the subject areas in all the skill sets. An example of this phenomenon is "Project Management Context." It simply involves reading and applying knowledge of the subject. That's all that's necessary. The subject tops out at level 2.

To summarize the interaction of the two tables, let's take one subject through from beginning to end.

Subject number "1" is the reference number. The subject is "Project Management Context." The subject is a Firm "F" skill type. The subject is defined as "The context within which a project is conceived, issued, conducted, and accepted." The definition of the subject can be enhanced or amplified by reading paragraph "2.0" of the PMI PMBOK, Topic "12" of the APM BOK, or Element "5" of the IPMA Competence Baseline. By adding the second table, we find that the basic level must have a thorough understanding of the subjects indicated and be able to apply an advanced level of knowledge, backed by appropriate experience, to the projects he or she is leading.

Now, let's look at the actual skill sets.

Basic Skill Set

Preparation for the Basic Skill Set involves a change of thinking from follower to leader and a knowledge of what projects are all about. Simply reading and understanding the literature I mention in the paragraphs that follow will provide the information needed for the Basic Skill Set. However, I recommend you also read the document shown under "Suggested Reading" for even more information.

Description

The basic-level manager will coordinate or supervise a single-disciplined task of low risk. The basic-level manager is responsible for applying the project management process (see Chapter 1) to ensure that the technical task is accomplished within the cost and schedule parameters established for the project.

Experience

One month to six months.

Subject Requirements

Figure 6-1 contains the primary subjects that constitute the Basic Skill Set. Each subject is followed by an abbreviated definition. You can expand these abbreviated definitions and that fundamental knowledge by reading James Lewis's *Fundamentals of Project Management*. This book will give you insight to all the subjects you need to know to conduct a small project. You can also review the documents referenced in the appropriate paragraphs of the Project Management Institute's *Project Management Body of Knowledge (PMBOK)* under the column labeled PMI. Should you desire further amplification of the subjects, refer to the two far-right columns. The column labeled APM will refer you to the topics of the *APM Project Management Body of Knowledge (APM BOK)* and the column labeled ICB will refer you to the elements of the *IPMA Competence Baseline (ICB)*. You can find these documents referenced at "Suggested Reading" under the Advanced Skill Set.

Proficiency Requirements

Figure 6-2 contains the subjects, ordered by reference number (top row), and the proficiency requirements (bottom row) that the basic-level manager must achieve in order to operate efficiently at this level. Basic-level subjects are shown in bold.

Proficiency Enhancements

The world of project management is wide open to you at this point so you can leverage the basic-level subjects with any of the subjects in any of the levels that follow.

You can expand these abbreviated definitions and that fundamental knowledge by reading the *Fundamentals of Project Management*.

Resources

Without a doubt, the PMI's PMBOK provides all the subjects required for this level as well as the next. Read and understand the PMBOK

Figure 6-1. Basic-Level Skill Set.

No.	Subject	Skill Type	Abbreviated Definition	PMI	APM	ICB
1	Project Management Context	F	The context within which a project is conceived, issued, conducted, and accepted.	2.0	12	5
2	Project/Program Management Process	F	Management of the scope, cost, schedule, and quality of a specific task.	3.0	10 & 11	1
3	Work Content and Scope Management	F	Management of project content (deliverables).	5.0	30	13
4	Time Scheduling/ Phasing	F	Developing and applying the time necessary for accomplishment of individual activities and linking those activities to portray a project.	6.0	31	14
5	Budgeting & Cost Management	F	Defining project element "should cost" and managing activities to ensure those costs are controlled.	7.0	33	16
6	Project Implementation	F	Application of the project plan to the task at hand.	2.1.2	63	2
7	Project Close Out	F	The process of concluding a project, delivering the product to the customer and returning the resources to the enterprise. Also called "Hand-Over."	12.6	65	11

Skill Type. Where: F = Firm; S = Soft; C = Combination of F and S.

Figure 6-2. Basic-Level proficiency requirements.

1	**2**	**3**	**4**	**5**	**6**	**7**	8	9	10	11	12	13	14	15	16	17	18	19	20	21	22	23	24
2	**2**	**2**	**2**	**2**	**2**	**2**	1	1	1	1	1	1	1	1	1	1	1	1	1	1	1	1	1

25	26	27	28	29	30	31	32	33	34	35	36	37	38	39	40	41	42	43	44	45	46	47
1	1	1	1	1	1	1	1	1	1	1	1	1	1	1	1	1	1	1	—	—	—	—

Bold numbers indicate Subject Areas and proficiency requirements specific to this level.

Proficiency requirements. Where: 1 = Understands; 2 = Applies Basic knowledge; 3 = Applies Advanced knowledge; 4 = Applies Expert knowledge; 5 = Delegates and controls.

(Project Management Institute, 2000) knowledge areas and meet the limited experience requirements to get ready for the basic level.

In *Fundamentals of Project Management*, James Lewis applies the knowledge areas of the PMBOK to real-world exercises. For example, his Chapter 6, "Scheduling Project Work," applies to PMBOK knowledge area 6, "Time Management." His Chapter 4, "Using the Work Breakdown Structure to Plan a Project," is a combination of parts of PMBOK knowledge area 4, "Project Integration Management," and PMBOK knowledge area 5, "Scope Management." These two books should be read together. Any seminar listed in any of the skill sets will be great but none is necessary for this level.

Suggested Reading

Dixon, Miles, ed. *APM Project Management Body of Knowledge.* Peterborough, U.K.: The Association for Project Management, 2000.

International Project Management Association. *IPMA Competence Baseline.* Monmouth, U.K.: International Project Management Association, 1999.

Lewis, James. *Fundamentals of Project Management.* New York: AMACOM Books, 2001.

Project Management Institute. *PMI PMBOK.* Newtown Square, Penn.: Project Management Institute, 2000.

Advanced Skill Set

In Figure 4-1, we saw that an advanced-level project manager must be able to lead both intermediate projects and large projects. These project types differ from the small project in the numbers of people involved, the complexity of the project, and the potential risk of the project. Therefore, the skill set of the advanced-level project manager must be expanded to include the skills necessary to accomplish these expanded tasks.

Projects with more team members will require more people-related subjects such as personnel management, organization (regarding the team organization), team building, and training. The larger and more complex projects need more attention to their composition and are subject to more changes than simpler projects. Therefore subjects such as project life cycle, organization (relating to product organization), configuration management, and change control must be added to the skills inventory. The control of risk is augmented by the subjects just mentioned as well as the use of a more rigorous control system such as earned value management.

The advanced level is the point at which the individual manager's persona begins to emerge. The AIPM, APM, asapm, and the IPMA include this fact in their certification process. They call it "attitude." But, because the current street jargon defines "attitude" as a negative attribute, I have chosen to use Jung's term "persona." Persona comes from the Greek actor's vocabulary and means how one is perceived. Believe me, how you are perceived is 90 percent of life, maybe even more. It's not just an act, though, it has a purpose, such as being able to smile when you really want to tear out someone's windpipe. This action would not solve the problem, would be detrimental to the performance of the project, and certainly would not do his windpipe any good. How you handle this kind of situation constitutes your persona and how you are perceived. The two ends of the persona spectrum can be referred to as the "Raging Bull" and "Cool Hand Luke."

Description

The advanced-level project manager will lead a multidisciplined team to achieve a task of moderate risk and moderate complexity. In addition to cost, schedule, and scope management, the advanced project manager now has the responsibility for selecting team members and ensuring that they understand the project and its objectives. The advanced-level project manager will interpret the task requirements, and create, implement, and manage a complex project plan that ensures that all requirements are met and all deliverables accrue to the customer at the proper times with appropriate quality.

Experience

One to three years, depending on the complexity of the project.

Subject Requirements

Figure 6-3 contains the subjects that constitute the advanced-level skill set. Each subject is followed by an abbreviated definition. The abbreviated definitions can be expanded by reviewing the documents referenced in the columns headed PMI, APM, and ICB. PMI refers to the Project Management Institute's *Project Management Body of Knowledge (PMBOK)*. APM refers to the topics of the *APM Project Management Body of Knowledge (APM BOK)*. ICB refers to the elements of the *IPMA Competence Baseline (ICB)*.

Proficiency Requirements

Figure 6-4 contains the subjects, ordered by reference number (top row), and the proficiency requirements (bottom row) that the advanced-

(text continues on page 56)

Figure 6-3. Advanced-Level Skill Set.

Ref. No.	Subject	Skill	Abbreviated Definition	PMI	APM	ICB
8	Project Success Criteria	C	The objective factors that define project success.	—	20	9
9	Strategy/Project Management Planning	C	The process of developing a project plan that is consistent with enterprise and customer requirements.	4.0	21	4 & 8
10	Communication	C	Two-way oral, written, or graphic interchange of data between people and/or machines.	10.0	70	25
11	Resource Management	F	Definition and control of the facilities, finances, equipment, and real estate in support of a project.	7.1	32	15
12	Change Control	F	Management of changes to *project* content.	4.3	34 & 41	17
13	Information Management	F	Management of the flow of information into, within, and out of the project.	10.0	36	21 & 29
14	Structures	F	Organization of project activities to show relationships between the elements of the activities, such as a Work Breakdown Structure (WBS).	2.3, 5.3 & 9.1.3	30 & 66	12
15	Configuration Management	F	Management of changes to the *product* baseline.	4.3.2.2	46	17 & 37

(continues)

Figure 6-3. (Continued).

Ref. No.	Subject	Skill	Abbreviated Definition	PMI	APM	ICB
16	Project Life Cycle Design & Management	F	Determination of the lifecycle a project is to have and then developing a plan to ensure accomplishment.	2.1	40, 60 & 61	6 & 10
17	Procurements & Subcontracts	F	The processes of buying products and services from other entities.	12.0	53	27
18	Earned Value Management	F	A process that assigns value to events. The predetermined value is then awarded to the performer whenever the event is completed.	4.1.4	35	19
19	Organization	C	A structured relationship between the people of the project at a particular moment in time.	23.3	66 & 67	22 & 33
20	Risk Management	C	Identification and control of risks that could affect the project.	11.0	23	18
21	Quality Management	C	Management of the quality processes of a project.	8.0	24	28
22	Personnel Management	C	Evaluating personnel needs, the recruiting and assignment of personnel, and the evaluation of the performance of those personnel.	9.0	75	35
23	Team Building/ Teamwork	C	Processes by which people work together for the common good of the project rather than individual desires.	9.3	71	23
24	Training	C	Exposing individuals to selected, *project-related* courses.	9.3.5	75	35 & 36

Skill Type. Where: F = Firm; S = Soft; C = Combination of F and S.

Figure 6-4. Advanced-Level proficiency requirements.

1	2	3	4	5	6	7	**8**	**9**	**10**	**11**	**12**	**13**	**14**	**15**	**16**	**17**	**18**	**19**	**20**	**21**	**22**	**23**	**24**
3	2	3	2	3	3	3	**3**	**3**	**3**	**3**	**3**	**3**	**3**	**3**	**3**	**3**	**3**	**3**	**3**	**3**	**3**	**3**	**5**

25	26	27	28	29	30	31	32	33	34	35	36	37	38	39	40	41	42	43	44	45	46	47
2	2	2	2	2	2	2	2	2	2	2	2	1	1	1	1	2	2	3	—	—	—	—

Bold numbers indicate Subject Areas and proficiency requirements specific to this level.

Proficiency requirements. Where: 1 = Understands; 2 = Applies Basic knowledge; 3 = Applies Advanced knowledge; 4 = Applies Expert knowledge; 5 = Delegates and controls.

level manager must achieve in order to operate efficiently at this level. Advanced-level subjects are shown in bold.

Proficiency Enhancement Resources

Now, it's time for you to broaden your effectiveness and work on your persona. The time-honored book *The 7 Habits of Highly Effective People* by Stephen R. Covey is a good place to start. It is a break from the regimen of book after book of the "Firm" subjects to a look at the personal habits by which others judge you. The book presents explanations of "Dependence" and the transition to "Independence" and then to "Interdependence." This book introduced the concepts of teamwork and synergy. And its ideas are just as effective today as the day it was written.

Ken Blanchard wrote the original *The One-Minute Manager* in 1981 and updated the book in 1999. Its three principles are as relevant now as they were then. However, the book has been further updated for the times in his newer book *Leadership and the One-Minute Manager*. In this book, Blanchard talks about the one-minute manager and situational leadership attuned to today's strategies. It is likely we will cycle back through all those strategies in the near future.

Gung Ho! expands the management techniques of *The One-Minute Manager* to include the concept of energizing and empowering the modern employee.

In his book, *The AMA Handbook of Project Management*, Dr. Paul C. Dinsmore pulls together the talents of forty-one respected practitioners of project management to contribute their expertise, each in a selected subject. The book covers the subjects you would expect, such as start-up, structure and organizations, teamwork, and quality, and also covers such subjects as research and development projects, new products, and cross-cultural projects. It will have a place on your project management bookshelf for years to come.

In his book *Introduction to Simulation and Risk Analysis*, James R. Evans uses the Excel spreadsheet as a teaching and operational tool to illustrate simulation modeling concepts and analysis of results. Excel is a tool common to almost every office software set and can be used in direct support of your project.

Tom Harris wrote *I'm OK, You're OK* during the Transactional Analysis phase of management techniques. This little book contains some basic people-to-people relationships that are almost immediately recognizable but heretofore didn't have names. The book became the starting point for several comedic spin-offs (*I'm OK, But I Don't Know About You*), but nevertheless it has a lot to say.

Written for both team leaders and executives, Glen M. Parker's *Cross-Functional Teams* provides checklists and sample training programs to help establish effective teams. His data is based on his consulting experiences with many large and medium businesses and will help you in your search for the right training courses for your projects.

The following seminars and subject areas are recommended for this level.

The PMI seminar "Contracting and Procurement Management" covers the procurement process from start to negotiation and award, then through performance and completion for project managers to understand their roles as well as the roles of procurement personnel.

The PMI "Risk Management" workshop uses an array of practical management tools to build risk models for standard risk identification, quantification, qualification, response development, and risk control. The idea is to establish a common approach that can be used for all projects, not just one.

The AMA seminar "Effective Project Leadership: Building High Commitment Through Superior Communication" covers not only basic communication but the specifics of team dynamics and conflict management as well. The seminar covers communicating during project planning, implementation and closure and the "nits and grits" of running effective meetings, what to do when crisis hits, performance reporting, and building commitment to the project.

Suggested Reading

Allen, David. *Getting Things Done: The Art of Stress Free Productivity*. New York: Penguin, 2003.

Australian National Training Authority Standards and Curriculum Council. *National Competency Standards for Project Management*. Volumes 1, 2, and 3. QLD, Australia: Yeronga, 1996.[1]

Blanchard, Ken. *Gung Ho!* New York: William Morrow, 1997.

———. *The One-Minute Manager*. New York: William Morrow, 1999.

Blanchard, Kenneth, et al. *Leadership and the One-Minute Manager*. New York: William Morrow, 2001.

Christopher, William F., ed. *Handbook for Productivity Measurement and Improvement*. New York: Productivity Press, 1993.

Covey, Stephen R. *The 7 Habits of Highly Effective People*. New York: Simon and Schuster, 1990.

Dinsmore, Paul C. *AMA Handbook of Project Management*. New York: AMACOM Books, 1993.

Dixon, Miles, ed. *APM Project Management Body of Knowledge*. Peterborough, U.K.: Association for Project Management, 2000.[2]

Evans, James R., and David L. Olson. *Introduction to Simulation and Risk Analysis*. Upper Saddle River, N.J.: Prentice Hall, 1998.

Harris, Thomas A. *I'm OK, You're OK*. New York: Avon Books, 1996.

International Project Management Association. *IPMA Competence Baseline*, Monmouth. U.K.: International Project Management Association, 1999.[3]

MacKenzie, R. Alec. *The Time Trap: The Classic Book on Time Management, 3rd Edition*. New York: AMACOM Books, 1997.

Parker, Glen M. *Cross-Functional Teams*. San Francisco: Jossey Bass, 2003.

Project Management Institute. *PMI PMBOK*. Newtown Square, Penn.: Project Management Institute, 2000.[4]

Seminar Contacts

Contracting and Procurement Management
PMI SeminarsWorld Registration
P.O. Box 2686
Des Plaines, IL 60018 USA
For a summary of the seminar, see:
http://www.pmi.org/prod/groups/public/documents/info/pdc_sw_reginfo.asp

Risk Management
Mailing address same as above.
For a summary of the seminar, see:
http://www.pmi.org/prod/groups/public/documents/info/pdc_sw_td_risk.asp

Effective Project Leadership: Building High Commitment Through Superior Communication—Seminar #6585-XNET
American Management Association
1601 Broadway New York, NY 10019
Phone: 212 586-8100
Fax: 212 903-8168
Customer Service: 800 262-9699
For a summary of the seminar, see:
http://www.amanet.org/seminars/cmd2/6585.htm

Expert Skill Set

The principal difference between the Advanced Skill Set and the Expert Skill Set is that at the expert level, the manager is involved with customers outside the enterprise under the aegis of a legal contract that binds the enterprise to the performance of the program. The expert-level manager must now add business and contractual subjects to his or her skills inventory. In many cases this also includes sales techniques and proposal preparation. Now that you are interfacing with a customer from outside the company, you should be more precise in handling your customer, not only from a profit standpoint but from a follow-on business standpoint as well.

Description

The expert-level manager leads programs of moderate to high risk and complexity and may be involved in several programs simultaneously. The expert-level manager is responsible for program budget and schedule as well as program technical performance. The expert-level manager leads an interdisciplinary staff and team. The expert-level manager is responsible for profit or loss. The expert-level manager is the primary customer contact, is responsible for customer satisfaction, and may be responsible for follow-on business. Follow-on business activity may involve writing and managing proposals, arranging for partnerships and teammates, and negotiating or leading the negotiating team.

Experience

Two to five years, depending on complexity.

Subject Requirements

Figure 6-5 contains the subjects that constitute the expert skill set. Each subject is followed by an abbreviated definition. The abbreviated definitions can be expand by reviewing the documents referenced in the columns headed PMI, APM, and ICB. PMI refers to the Project Management Institute's *Project Management Body of Knowledge (PMBOK)*. APM refers to the topics of the *APM Project Management Body of Knowledge (APM BOK)*. ICB refers to the elements of the *IPMA Competence Baseline (ICB)*.

Proficiency Requirements

Figure 6-6 contains the subjects, ordered by reference number (top row), and the proficiency requirements (bottom row) that the expert-level manager must achieve in order to operate efficiently at this level. Expert-level subjects are shown in bold.

(text continues on page 64)

Figure 6-5. Expert-Level Skill Set.

Ref. No.	Subject	Skill	Abbreviated Definition	PMI	APM	ICB
25	Financial Management	F	The evaluation and assignment of resources to a project as opposed to the assignment of those resources to alternatives.	12.5	52	42
26	Metrics (TPM)	F	Objective values applied to certain factors and accomplishments.	8.1.3.2	21	19
27	Value Management	F	Assessing project value in terms of resource utilization (Go/No-Go).	5.1.1.3	44	20
28	Health, Safety, Security & Environment	F	Considerations of the health, safety, security, and environment for the *project*.	5.1.3.3	25	40
29	Business Considerations	C	How this project fits in the overall business plan of the enterprise and how it will contribute to future business. Uses the elements of the project success criteria.	1.2	50	34
30	Design & Development	C	Establishing key management "Go/No Go" gates in the design and development processes.	2.1.1	22, 60 & 62	7, 38 & 39

31	Legal Considerations	C	The ability to recognize a situation outside the norm that will require specialized assistance, such as labor, commercial, or international law.	1.4, 5.5.2, 11.2.1.3 & 12.4	54	41
32	Technology Management	C	An enterprise-level plan that predicts new technologies and follows their direction of growth. Used by the project to ensure that "on-ramps" or accommodations are made to implement predictions.	2.1	43	12
33	Estimating	C	A process of assigning approximate value, based on like activities, to a projected activity.	7.2.2.1	42	15 & 16
34	Prototyping	C	Developing a living model that reflects the characteristics of the product to be delivered.	11.5.2.3	45	31
35	Handoff	C	The transfer of a requirement from one functional organization (marketing) to another (programs).	—	—	—
36	Customer Relations/ Satisfaction	S	Documents the needs and wants of the project customer and establishes a periodic evaluation of performance in meeting those needs and wants.	8.0	—	—

(continues)

Figure 6-5. (Continued).

Ref. No.	Subject	Skill	Abbreviated Definition	PMI	APM	ICB
37	Teaming & Partnering	S	A strategic or tactical alliance with another enterprise for a specific purpose.	2.3	53	27
38	Marketing & Sales	S	That part of the permanent organization chartered to sell product and ideas between the enterprise and its customers.	1.4	51	38
39	Proposals	S	A process that generates an offer to do business that usually consists of scope, schedule and cost/ price, and approach.	12.3	—	—
40	Negotiation	S	A discussion in which there is ultimately agreement on the outcome of the subject of the discussion.	2.4.3	74	32
41	Conflict Management	S	Mediating a dispute to a positive conclusion before it becomes disruptive.	2.4	73	26
42	Social Sensitivity	S	Acting, speaking, and writing in a manner that is considerate of the needs of others.	2.5	50	9
43	Management Relations/ Satisfaction	S	Establishing and satisfying project goals between enterprise management and project management.	2.2	—	—

Skill Type. Where: F = Firm; S = Soft; C = Combination of F and S.

Figure 6-6. Expert-Level proficiency requirements.

1	2	3	4	5	6	7	8	9	10	11	12	13	14	15	16	17	18	19	20	21	22	23	24
2	4	4	4	4	4	4	4	4	4	4	4	4	4	4	4	4	4	4	4	3	3	4	5

25	**26**	**27**	**28**	**29**	**30**	**31**	**32**	**33**	**34**	**35**	**36**	**37**	**38**	**39**	**40**	**41**	**42**	**43**	44	45	46	47
4	**4**	**4**	**5**	**3**	**3**	**2**	**2**	**3**	**3**	**4**	**4**	**4**	**4**	**4**	**4**	**3**	**3**	**4**	4	2	—	1

Bold numbers indicate Subject Areas and proficiency requirements specific to this level.

Proficiency requirements. Where: 1 = Understands; 2 = Applies Basic knowledge; 3 = Applies Advanced knowledge; 4 = Applies Expert knowledge; 5 = Delegates and controls.

Proficiency Enhancement

In addition to achieving the specific proficiency requirements shown in Figure 6-6 you can leverage your proficiency at the expert level by reading the following books and attending the following seminars.

Resources

Change your customers from simply being satisfied customers into *Raving Fans* by using Ken Blanchard's ideas that teach how to define a vision, to learn what a customer really wants, and to institute constant, effective customer-centered systems.

Use my *Blueprint for Project Recovery* to recover from a problem on your project or program, or to control the planning so you don't have issues to recover from.

How you handle change is really the subject of Spencer Johnson's *Who Moved My Cheese?* Just about the time you have the "cheese" (rewards) figured out, someone moves them. The concepts are applicable to the business world and to one's personal life.

Just mention "risk" and watch the eyeballs of the project manager snap. Risk is inherent to all projects and compounds exponentially as projects become more and more complex. In *Identifying and Managing Project Risk,* Tom Kendrick addresses risk from an overall project standpoint and provides a base from which you can move to your specialty. It appears to me that risk is the most addressed subject in the project management list of subjects. Every month, articles about risk appear in all the periodicals. Software has even been developed to assist the project manager in identifying and controlling risk. Still in all, risk exists in every project and must be controlled, and this is a good place to start.

Even though the book is titled for small business, *Successful Proposal Strategies for Small Business* by Robert Frey provides insight to proposal strategies for almost all sizes of companies and most of the agencies you can think of from concept to printing.

Managing the Project Team is Vijay Verma's third volume in "The Human Aspects of Project Management Series" and covers team dynamics, inspiring performance, and creating self-motivating project teams.

At this point in your project management career, you should have covered just about all of the "Firm" subjects. Now is the time to add depth to the firm subjects, concentrate on the "Soft" subjects and to work on your persona. Most of the seminars recommended at this level are a combination of subject areas (that is, not single subjects) and lean more to the human or people side of the business.

Team Training. There are many approaches to team training but *Agreements for Excellence* uses a "contract" or "agreement" between team members as the basis for understanding what is needed by who and when. Each team member "signs up" to provide certain products to others at certain times. There are usually surprises in every project when people find out they are supposed to provide a product they didn't even know about before. I use *Agreements for Excellence,* presented by qualified facilitators, in all my team training seminars.

Contract Types Workshop. If a contract with an outside agency is part of your task, you need to understand the different types of contracts and what each means to you, to the customer, and to the company. Nearly all of the project management graduate curricula (see Chapter 7) offer courses in contract types, and that's a good starting point for information. There are some nuances of contract types that are industry-specific. For instance, a cost-plus contract in construction is not the same as a cost-plus contract with the federal government, so you need to select the course that supports the industry you are in. Further, the fee aspects (profit) of some contracts such as fixed fee (FF), award fee (AF), and incentive fee (IF) can be particularly complex and will require detailed knowledge of the award or incentive factors. These details are usually spelled out in the specific contract under which you will be working.

Defective Pricing. Defective pricing falls under the general heading of fraud, waste, and abuse. Requirements for project managers to be exposed to the definitions and penalties for defective pricing was begun by the U.S. federal government in the 1960s. Many other organizations have made this a requirement as well. These seminars are usually developed by companies around their pricing practices.

Negotiating. Since 1968, *Effective Negotiating* has been the standard for negotiating strategies and techniques. In his *Effective Negotiating* seminar, Dr. Chester L. Karrass states: "They get what they want by negotiating better deals for both parties."[5] This is the basis for win-win negotiations.

Proposals. New business, and, by association, proposals, are the lifeblood of any company. There are many, many proposal types, but the proposal must match the requirements. You don't want to write a book when one page will do, and you don't want to submit one page when a full-blown proposal is required. Usually, the training department will select a proposal seminar, so proposals will be standardized throughout the company. If you are in commercial business, *Writing Commercial Proposals* is a good seminar. If you are in the government business, *Managing Winning Proposals* is the appropriate seminar. Both are offered by Shipley Associates.

Suggested Reading

Blanchard, Ken. *Raving Fans*. New York: William Morrow, 1993.

Blanchard, Kenneth, and Spencer Johnson. *The One-Minute Manager*. New York: William Morrow, 1999.

Cagle, Ronald B. *Blueprint for Project Recovery*. New York: AMACOM Books, 2003.

Frey, Robert. *Successful Proposal Strategies for Small Business: Using Knowledge Management to Win Government, Private-Sector, and International Contracts, 3rd Edition*. Boston: Artech House Publishers, 2002.

Humphrey, Watt S. *Managing Technical People*. Boston: Addison-Wesley, 1996.

Johnson, Spencer. *Who Moved My Cheese?* New York: Putnam Books, 1998.

Kendrick, Tom. *Identifying and Managing Project Risk: Essential Tools for Failure-Proofing Your Project*. New York: AMACOM Books, 2003.

Verma, Vijay, K. *Managing the Project Team the Human Aspects of Project Management*. Newtown Square, Penn.: Project Management Institute, 1997.

Seminar Contacts

Agreements for Excellence
Created by and offered through:
IMPAQ Organizational Improvement Systems, East Coast Division
45 Museum Street, Suite C
Cambridge, MA, 02138
Phone: 617 354-5062

Effective Negotiating seminar
Karrass Corporation
8370 Wilshire Blvd.
Beverly Hills, CA 90211–USA
Phone: 323 951-7500
E-mail: mail@karrass.com
Web site: www.karrass.com

Writing Commercial Proposals and *Managing Winning Proposals*
Shipley Associates
Corporate Headquarters
653 North Main St.
Farmington, UT 84025
Phone: 888 772-9467 or 801 451-2323
Fax: 801 451-4660
Web site: www.shipleywins.com

Specialty Skill Set

The specialty project manager is an advanced-level manager or an expert-level manager with an added specialization in a specific area. Specialty projects may include new technology or new product development and may be international in scope or application. Specialty projects or programs may be "virtual" and may encompass several locations, including overseas locations.

Description

The specialist-level manager leads projects or programs of moderate to high risk and complexity, manages an interdisciplinary staff, and may be involved in several projects or programs simultaneously. The specialist-level manager is responsible for project or program budget, schedule, and technical performance. The specialist-level manager usually acts as primary customer contact, is responsible for customer satisfaction, and may be responsible for follow-on business.

Experience

Five to ten years.

Subject Requirements

Figure 6-7 contains the subjects that constitute the specialty-level skill set. Each subject is followed by an abbreviated definition. Specialty-level subject areas include specific areas of interest or responsibility, such as leading virtual teams, conducting international business, working with AID (Agency for International Development), and so on, but in truth, there is no end to the category of specialties.

Proficiency Requirements

Figure 6-8 contains the proficiency requirements of the specialist-level subjects, by reference number (top row), and the proficiency requirements (bottom row), that the specialist-level manager must achieve in order to operate efficiently at this level. Primary subjects are shown in bold.

Proficiency Enhancement

Because the specialty area is so broad, you will see an admixture of subjects presented here. In truth, these subjects need to be whatever you need to support your specialty. That's not a cop-out, it's just reality, and when you reach this level, you will have no difficulty "filling in the blanks."

Resources

How to Negotiate Anything with Anyone, Anywhere Around the World by Frank L. Acuff presents in-depth information for international negotiat-

(text continues on page 70)

Figure 6-7. Specialist-Level Skill Set.

No.	Subject	Skill Type	Abbreviated Definition	PMI	APM	ICB
44	Specialties	C	Numerous categories of specialty subjects, such as international business, AID business, Foreign Military Sales, and virtual programs.	—	—	—

Skill Type. Where: F = Firm; S = Soft; C = Combination of F and S.

Figure 6-8. Specialist-Level proficiency requirements.

1	2	3	4	5	6	7	8	9	10	11	12	13	14	15	16	17	18	19	20	21	22	23	24
2	4	4	4	4	4	4	4	4	4	4	4	4	4	4	4	4	4	4	4	5	4	4	5

25	26	27	28	29	30	31	32	33	34	35	36	37	38	39	40	41	42	43	**44**	45	46	47
4	4	4	5	3	3	3	3	3	3	4	4	4	4	4	4	3	3	4	**4**	2	—	2

Bold numbers indicate Subject Areas and proficiency requirements specific to this level.

Proficiency requirements. Where: 1 = Understands; 2 = Applies Basic knowledge; 3 = Applies Advanced knowledge; 4 = Applies Expert knowledge; 5 = Delegates and controls.

ing. The author separates the world into six regions consisting of forty-one countries and calls for different negotiating methods with each one. A "Fast-Fact Summary" is provided for each nation allowing the reader to quickly grasp the uniqueness of that country.

Aligned to conducting business around the globe, *The Distance Manager* by Kimball Fisher covers the main topics that a project manager must consider when using virtual teams through discussion of using e-mail, teleconferencing, and videoconferencing for maximum effectiveness; of mastering the people skills required to manage from a distance, of virtual team building, and of strategies for managing multiple locations.

Written more like a white paper than a book, Martha Haywood's *Managing Virtual Teams* nevertheless asks, and answers, all the right questions. For instance: What are the four key principles for effectively communicating at a distance? And, questions near and dear to the heart of all project managers: How do I know they are really working? How do I know they are working on the right things?

The selection of specialty seminars will be directed by the character of the specialty and will be numerous.

Suggested Reading

Acuff, Frank L. *How to Negotiate Anything with Anyone, Anywhere Around the World (Expanded Edition)*. New York: AMACOM Books, 1997.

Fisher, Kimball, and Mareen Duncan Fisher. *The Distance Manager: A Hands-On Guide to Managing Off-Site Employees and Virtual Teams.* New York: McGraw-Hill, 2000.

Haywood, Martha. *Managing Virtual Teams.* Boston: Artech House Publishers, 1998.

Principal Skill Set

The principal-level manager must be able to handle any project or program the enterprise has or will have. The task of the principal-level manager is entirely management-oriented; however, the principal-level manager must have an understanding of all the technical disciplines necessary to perform the project or program to ensure that it is on track. The task of the principal-level manager is strategic insofar as the program and the business area are concerned, and it is tactical insofar as the day-to-day activities are concerned. The detailed, day-to-day activities will be performed by staff specialists.

Description

The principal-level manager leads very complex and high-risk projects and programs. The principal-level manager oversees budget and schedules and directs an interdisciplinary staff. He or she has primary responsibility for program growth, including new technology. The principal-level manager is the primary customer contact and is responsible for customer satisfaction. Programs will likely include new technology and may include new product development. Programs may be international in scope or application. Portions of the projects or programs may be "virtual" and encompass several locations, including overseas locations. The principal-level manager is responsible for profit or loss. The principal-level manager will be responsible for follow-on business and may be responsible for new business. The principal-level manager will likely direct the marketing of the follow-on or new business activity.

Experience

More than ten years.

Subject Requirements

Figure 6-9 contains the subjects that constitute the Principal Skill Set. Each subject is followed by an abbreviated definition. As you can see, these subjects are beyond the scope of the Project Management Institute's *Project Management Body of Knowledge (PMBOK)*, the topics of the *APM Project Management Body of Knowledge (APM BOK)*, and the elements of the *IPMA Competence Baseline (ICB)* under the column labeled ICB. Note that the subject areas are purposely broad.

Proficiency Requirements

Figure 6-10 contains the proficiency requirements of the principal subjects, by reference number (top row), and the proficiency requirements (bottom row), that the principal-level manager must achieve in order to operate efficiently at this level. Principal subjects are shown in bold.

Proficiency Enhancement

In addition to achieving the specific proficiency requirements shown in Figure 6-10, you can leverage your proficiency at the expert level by reading the following books and attending the following seminars.

(text continues on page 74)

Figure 6-9. Principal-Level Skill Set.

No.	Subject	Skill Type	Abbreviated Definition	PMI	APM	ICB
45	Strategic Planning and Positioning	C	Developing and implementing the strategy for long-term positioning of the project, the program, and the enterprise. Includes cultural changes and continuous improvement.	—	—	—
46	Project Management Process implementation	C	The research and application of the Project Management Process to the needs of the enterprise.	—	—	—
47	Leading-Edge Ideas	S	Ideas put forth by management and technical sources specializing in forward thinking. Knowledge Management.	—	—	—

Skill Type. Where: F = Firm; S = Soft; C = Combination of F and S.

Figure 6-10. Principal-Level proficiency requirements.

1	2	3	4	5	6	7	8	9	10	11	12	13	14	15	16	17	18	19	20	21	22	23	24
4	4	4	5	5	4	4	4	4	4	4	5	5	5	5	5	5	5	4	4	5	5	5	5

25	26	27	28	29	30	31	32	33	34	35	36	37	38	39	40	41	42	43	44	**45**	**46**	**47**
4	5	4	4	4	4	4	4	5	5	4	4	4	4	4	4	4	4	4	5	**4**	**4**	**4**

Bold numbers indicate Subject Areas and proficiency requirements specific to this level.

Proficiency requirements. Where: 1 = Understands; 2 = Applies Basic knowledge; 3 = Applies Advanced knowledge; 4 = Applies Expert knowledge; 5 = Delegates and controls.

Resources

The project office is not only a way to conduct projects, it is also a way to conduct business. In their book *Creating the Project Office: A Manager's Guide to Leading Organizational Change,* Randall Englund, Robert Graham, and Paul Dinsmore suggest that the project office leads to better products, and can lead to organizational change by transforming the organization from function-based to project-based.

The authors interviewed over 150 CEOs to get the inside dope on how they run their companies. In *Maximum Leadership,* Charles Farkas and Phillippe DeBacker share the results of their interviews in five strategies for success.

Where do we stand with regard to others in our business? H. James Harrington's *High Performance Benchmarking* shows the "what's" and "how's" and how they come through in this first book on benchmarking.

Originally published by nine co-authors in 1996, this book has undergone editorial change by Miki Halliday and was republished in 2001. *Coaching, Mentoring, and Managing,* edited by William Hendricks, advocates treating your employees as real people and helping them along the way with coaching instead of condemning, and mentoring instead of maligning.

Robert S. Kaplan and David P. Norton bring their "balanced scorecard" concept from seminar to book form and extend it into a performance management framework in *The Strategy-Focused Organization.*

Business strategy with a practical application is the theme of *Strategic Planning: A Practical Guide for Managers,* by Drs. Harold Kerzner and Peter J. Rea. The authors use a dozen or more case studies to show how it's done in different companies.

Although Alvin Toffler's *The Third Wave* was written twenty years ago, it has as much thought-provoking insight as *Future Shock.* It is worth taking time to read it.

The "Reinventing Work Series" by Tom Peters consists of three books. The books are titled: *The Brand You 50, The Professional Firm 50,* and *The Project 50.* Each is a list of fifty actions to reinvent the work of that subject area. Naturally, we are most interested in *The Project 50* but the others are important as well.

Now for the seminars appropriate to the Principal Skill Set.

Appraise Your World was created by the Management Research Group of Portland, Maine. Where do your decision styles come from and how do they compare with a like group? Everyone is affected by a Professional/Public Self, Leisure Self, Personal Self, and Inner Self. Each of these factors includes four or five subfactors. The importance you place on each of these subfactors affects the way and ways you make decisions. *Appraise Your World* collects your response to these individual subfactors and compares them to a norm. The purpose is to give you an insight to how and why you make decisions and how you relate to your peers. Such inclinations will affect how you progress in your career, among other things.

The *Leadership Decision Styles Survey* was created by the Center for Creative Learning in Greensboro, North Carolina, and is usually presented by company training departments whom they certify in the process. Each company is franchised to handle the course. Using a series of case studies, the leader (you) decides how he or she will handle the decision required for each case by using one of the five methods as a basis. The results are analyzed by plotting your decision style against the recommended decision style for each case and then summed into a decision profile that represents you. The five decision styles form a spectrum, from making the decision alone to making a decision with the entire team involved.

Suggested Reading

Englund, Randall L., Robert J. Graham, and Paul C. Dinsmore. *Creating the Project Office: A Manager's Guide to Leading Organizational Change.* San Francisco: Jossey-Bass, 2003.

Farkas, Charles M., and Phillippe De Backer. *Maximum Leadership.* (New York: Perigee Books, 1998.

Harrington, H. James. *High Performance Benchmarking: 20 Steps to Success.* New York: McGraw-Hill Trade, 1995.

Hendricks, William, ed. *Coaching, Mentoring, and Managing.* Franklin Lakes, N.J.: The Career Press, Inc., 2001.

Kaplan, Robert S., and David P. Norton. *The Strategy-Focused Organization.* Boston: Harvard Business School Press, 2001.

Kerzner, Harold, and Peter J. Rea. *Strategic Planning: A Practical Guide for Managers.* New York: John Wiley and Sons, 1997.

Peters, Glen. *Beyond the Next Wave.* Englewood Cliffs, N.J.: Financial Times Prentice Hall, 1996.

Peters, Tom. *Reinventing Work Series.* New York: Alfred A. Knopf, 1999.

Toffler, Alvin. *The Third Wave.* New York: Bantam Books, 1984.

Seminar Contacts

Appraise Your World
Management Research Group

14 York Street, Suite 301
Phone: 207 775-2173
Fax: 207 775-6796
E-mail: Info@mrg.com
Web site: http://www.mrg.com

Leadership Decision Styles Survey
Center for Creative Leadership
One Leadership Place
P.O. Box 26300
Greensboro, NC 27438
Phone: 336 545-2810
Fax: 336 282-3284
E-mail: Info@Leaders.ccl.org
Web site: http://www.ccl.org

In this part we talked about the preparatory skills as well as the company, customer, and industry skills you need for project management. Then we went into each of the five levels and showed what subject areas were necessary to satisfy the needs of each level. We found that exposure to all the subject areas was desirable at every level but concentration on certain subject areas was essential in order to be competent at a specific level.

One thing I hope you learned in this part is that project management learning is progressive. It is progressive in both scope and depth. It is a learning process that never ends. This part presented those subject areas necessary for basic project management training and for getting a good start in expanding that basic training to advanced, expert, specialist, principal levels, and beyond.

Part III will build on this start and give you insight into more expertise through additional reading, workshops, and seminars.

Notes

1. Also available at: http://www.aipm.com.au/html/ncspm.cfm >Downloads (several).
2. Also available at: http://www.apm.org.uk/copyright/next.htm (document requires registration).
3. Also available at: http://www.ipma.ch/ >Certification >IPMA Competence Baseline Download.
4. For an excellent comparison of the PMI PMBoK and PRINCE2, see: http://www.pmforum.org/library/papers/Prince2vsGuide3.htm.
5. Dr. Chester L. Karrass, *Effective Negotiating* (New York: HarperBusiness, 1994), see: www.karrass.com.

IMPROVING YOUR PROJECT MANAGEMENT ABILITIES

"Good, Better, Best—Never let it rest—til' good is better, and better is best."[1] Although this quote has been used over and over again, it's still very timely. No matter where you are in your career, you need to keep abreast of what's going on. As Will Rogers said: "Even if you're on the right track, you'll get run over if you just sit there." So, we all must keep moving and improving. The intent of this part is to present an assessment tool that lists all the subject areas talked about in Part II, to be used as a checklist to make your self-assessment. Once you have made your assessment, you can see your strong points and your weak points. The action now is to assess where you are and create a plan for improving your position.

Note

1. Rev. William Long Dowler, First United Lutheran Church, 1948. Originator unknown.

CHAPTER 7

Expanding Your Knowledge

Expanding your knowledge is a good idea no matter what profession you are in, and you should constantly be putting effort into doing it. If you want to expand your knowledge in a specific area, however, it is a good idea to first take inventory of where you are. This chapter will recommend that you assess your capabilities in order to have an understanding of where you are now. Then you can expand your knowledge through education and training to where you want to be. Remember, knowledge is the first element of the Path to Success.

Assessing Your Capabilities

Now that you have an understanding for what is required for each level of proficiency, it is a good time to take inventory of your own skills and abilities. Below are five skill set tables (Figures 7-1 through 7-5) for evaluating your abilities. One table is provided for each skill set, and each subject area is provided with the nominal proficiency level needed for that subject. The nominal levels use the following taxonomy:

1. The individual must be able to apply the Basic Skill Set and have a proficiency of the remaining subjects as indicated.
2. The individual must have an advanced level of knowledge of the subjects indicated as well as all subjects in prior levels. This knowledge must be backed by appropriate experience on previous projects. The individual must be able to apply this knowledge and experience to the projects he or she is leading.
3. The individual must have an expert level of knowledge of the subjects indicated as well as all subjects in prior levels. This knowledge must be backed by appropriate experience on previ-

(text continues on page 88)

Figure 7-1. Basic Skill Set proficiency level.

No.	Subject	Skill Type	Abbreviated Definition	Standard	Your Proficiency
1	Project Management Context	F	The context within which a project is conceived, issued, conducted, and accepted.	2	
2	Project/Program Management Process	F	Management of the scope, cost, schedule, and quality of a specific task.	2	
3	Work Content and Scope Management	F	Management of project content (deliverables).	2	
4	Time Scheduling/ Phasing	F	Developing and applying the time necessary for accomplishment of individual activities and linking these activities to portray a project.	2	
5	Budgeting & Cost Management	F	Defining project element "should cost" and managing activities to ensure that those costs are controlled.	2	
6	Project Implementation	F	Application of the project plan to the task at hand.	2	
7	Project Close Out	F	The process of concluding a project, delivering the product to the customer, and returning the resources to the enterprise. Also called "Hand-Over."	2	

Skill Type. Where: F = Firm; S = Soft; C = Combination of F and S.

Figure 7-2. Advanced Skill Set proficiency levels.

No.	Subject	Skill Type	Abbreviated Definition	Standard	Your Proficiency
8	Project Success Criteria	C	The objective factors that define project success.	3	
9	Strategy/Project Management Planning	C	The process of developing a project plan that is consistent with enterprise and customer requirements.	3	
10	Communication	C	Two-way oral, written, or graphic interchange of data between people and/or machines.	3	
11	Resource Management	F	Definition and control of the facilities, finances, equipment, and real estate in support of a project.	3	
12	Change Control	F	Management of changes to *project* content.	3	
13	Information Management	F	Management of the flow of information into, within, and out of the project.	3	
14	Structures	F	Organization of project activities to show relationships between the elements of the activities, such as a Work Breakdown Structure (WBS).	3	
15	Configuration Management	F	Management of changes to the *product* baseline.	3	

(continues)

Figure 7-2. (Continued).

No.	Subject	Skill Type	Abbreviated Definition	Standard	Your Proficiency
16	Project Lifecycle Design & Management	F	Determination of the lifecycle a project is to have and then developing a plan to ensure accomplishment.	3	
17	Procurements & Subcontracts	F	The processes of buying products and services from other entities.	3	
18	Earned Value Management	F	A process that assigns value to events. The predetermined value is then awarded to the performer whenever the event is completed.	3	
19	Organization	C	A structured relationship between the people of the project at a particular moment in time.	3	
20	Risk Management	C	Identification and control of risks that could affect the project.	3	
21	Quality Management	C	Management of the quality processes of a project.	3	
22	Personnel Management	C	Evaluating personnel needs, the recruiting and assignment of personnel, and the evaluation of the performance of those personnel.	3	
23	Team Building/ Teamwork	C	Processes by which people work together for the common good of the project rather than individual desires.	3	
24	Training	C	Exposing individuals to selected *project-related* courses.	3	

Skill Type. Where: F = Firm; S = Soft; C = Combination of F and S.

Figure 7-3. Expert Skill Set proficiency levels.

No.	Subject	Skill Type	Abbreviated Definition	Standard	Your Proficiency
25	Financial Management	F	The evaluation and assignment of resources to a project as opposed to the assignment of those resources to alternatives.	4	
26	Metrics (TPM)	F	Objective values applied to certain factors and accomplishments.	4	
27	Value Management	F	Assessing project value in terms of resource utilization (Go/No Go).	4	
28	Health, Safety, Security, & Environment	F	Considerations of the health, safety, security, and environment for the *project*.	5	
29	Business Considerations	C	How this project fits in the overall business plan of the enterprise and how it will contribute to future business. Uses the elements of the project success criteria.	3	
30	Design & Development	C	Establishing key management, "Go/No Go" gates in the design and development processes.	3	

(continues)

Figure 7-3. (Continued).

No.	Subject	Skill Type	Abbreviated Definition	Standard	Your Proficiency
31	Legal Considerations	C	The ability to recognize a situation outside the norm that will require specialized assistance such as labor, commercial, or international law.	2	
32	Technology Management	C	An enterprise-level plan that predicts new technologies and follows their direction of growth. Used by the project to ensure that "on-ramps" or accommodations are made to implement predictions.	2	
33	Estimating	C	A process of assigning approximate value, based on like activities, to a projected activity.	3	
34	Prototyping	C	Developing a living model that reflects the characteristics of the product to be delivered.	3	
35	Handoff	C	The transfer of a requirement from one functional organization (marketing) to another (programs).	4	
36	Customer Relations/ Satisfaction	S	Documents the needs and wants of the project customer and establishes a periodic evaluation of performance in meeting those needs and wants.	4	
37	Teaming & Partnering	S	A strategic or tactical alliance with another enterprise for a specific purpose.	4	

38	Marketing & Sales	S	That part of the permanent organization chartered to sell product and ideas between the enterprise and its customers.	4	
39	Proposals	S	A process that generates an offer to do business that usually consists of scope, schedule, and cost/price, approach.	4	
40	Negotiation	S	A discussion in which there is ultimately agreement on the outcome of the subject of the discussion.	4	
41	Conflict Management	S	Mediating a dispute to a positive conclusion before it becomes disruptive.	3	
42	Social Sensitivity	S	Acting, speaking, and writing in a manner that is considerate of the needs of others.	3	
43	Management Relations/Satisfaction	S	Establishing and satisfying project goals between enterprise management and project management.	4	

Skill Type. Where: F = Firm; S = Soft; C = Combination of F and S.

Figure 7-4. Specialist Skill Set proficiency levels.

No.	Subject	Skill Type	Abbreviated Definition	Standard	Your Proficiency
44	Specialties	C	Numerous categories of specialty subjects, such as international business, AID business, foreign military sales, and virtual programs.	4	

Skill Type. Where: F = Firm; S = Soft; C = Combination of F and S.

Figure 7-5. Principal Skill Set proficiency levels.

No.	Subject	Skill Type	Abbreviated Definition	Standard	Your Proficiency
45	Strategic Planning and Positioning	C	Developing and implementing the strategy for long-term positioning of the project, the program, and the enterprise.	4	
46	Project Management Office Implementation	C	The development and implementation of a properly reasoned, sized, and organized project or program management office.	4	
47	Leading-Edge Ideas	S	Ideas put forth by management and technical sources specializing in forward thinking. Knowledge Management.	4	

Skill Type. Where: F = Firm; S = Soft; C = Combination of F and S.

ous projects. The individual must be able to apply this knowledge and experience to the projects he or she is leading.

4. The individual must have an advanced or expert level of knowledge of the subjects indicated as well as of all subjects in prior levels. The individual must be an expert in the specialty required by the project and must have appropriate experience on previous projects. The individual must be able to apply this knowledge and experience to the projects he or she is leading.
5. The individual at this level must be an expert in all subjects. Much of the detail level of the subjects will be delegated to subordinates, but this individual must fully understand the subject area, approve the subject delegation, and be responsible for the resulting product.

Take a few minutes to fill in the far-right column and give yourself a baseline of where you stand. Then we will be ready to talk about improving your abilities in all the areas.

Now you should be able to see where you excel and where you need to improve. But simply meeting the standards won't be sufficient as you progress through your career. Remember the opening line—"Good, Better, Best." You will want to increase the level of each subject area as you progress in your career. The next section of this chapter offers some insight into how and where you can do just that.

Expanding Your Knowledge

Knowledge, as I said before, is a combination of education and training. Education consists of formal courses given by accredited educational institutions such as colleges and universities. The first part of this chapter will address formal education.

Training is offered in both formal and informal environments, but training does not lead to a degree in any field. Formal training usually culminates in a certificate or some similar type of recognition. Training will be discussed in the second part of this chapter.

Certification is offered by some project management organizations, and important enough to discuss separately.

Expanding Your Education

There are a few questions to consider before expanding your education: Where are you now in your education? What career field do you want to consider? What level of that career field do you want to enter? In what location do you want to go to school? What particular school do you want to go to? Do you want to go to school full-time, part-time, day, night, correspondence, via e-learning? How will you pay for your schooling?

Let's take the questions one by one and give them enough specificity to get you started on your search.

Where Are You Now in Your Education?

The answer to this question will vector you to the level you would like to achieve next.

If you are in high school, the whole world is potentially open to you. The breadth of these options begins to narrow immediately by the next set of considerations: Do you have the GPA to achieve your dream, and do you have the financing to do what you want to do? These two questions are the most basic in pursuing your education. If you do not have an appropriate GPA (and SAT) to go into your chosen field, you may have a problem. I hope you are reading and heeding this early in your career when you have time to overcome the problem. If you do not have the appropriate GPA for College A, you may be accepted by College B, or if not there, you may able to attend Community College C and then transfer to the upper division of State College D. This is not the best way to get there, but it will work.

If you are at the undergraduate level, you essentially have two choices: Go into the workplace or continue on to get your undergraduate degree. If you choose to go on with your undergraduate program, you need to decide what career field you want to go into? It is after primary education is established that most people go into project management, and that's the baseline we will use to approach this career question. So if you are looking at your undergraduate field, that field will be your primary field. Your primary field may be computer science, chemical engineering, finance, banking, construction, or dozens of other fields. Whatever it is, you must make a careful consideration at this point. You need to enter at least the general field you want to pursue.

Granted, you don't need to make your final commitment to a major before entering your freshman year of college but you must make that decision before entering your junior year (upper division) of college. Why? Because if you don't, you will spend a lot of time unproductively, when you should be making progress toward your goals. If you choose incorrectly and then want to change later, you may have amassed (and paid for) college hours that are of no use to your new major. Granted, education is never wasted, but if it doesn't apply directly to your major, you will be taking time away from your final career choice.

The most important point to research in choosing a college is the accreditation of the program and the college. There are many programs that are offered and look good, but that are not accredited by an acceptable source. I recommend that you avoid these kinds of programs.

If you are near the end of your undergraduate program, you once again have the option of going into the workforce or going into a graduate program. At this point, you may have a watershed. By this I mean, you may continue on at the graduate level with your primary career field or you may change career fields. At this point you are probably asking: "Why is this guy talking about changing a career field when he's been preaching stay the course all along?" Good question. But, this is the point when you determine whether you want to stay operating in your primary field, go into management of your primary field, or go into project management at the graduate level. That's the purpose. Naturally, you can choose to extend your primary career field and become expert there. Or, you can choose the management option and change to an MBA or a master's degree in Project Management. If you have been in some related field—say, finance—and want to get an MBA, you can probably go directly into your graduate program. If, on the other hand, you choose to change your field from, say, electrical engineering to management, you will probably need to take some prerequisite courses to make the change. These prerequisites will likely be undergraduate courses at the 200 to 400 level. This is part of the tax you pay whenever you change majors. In some cases, you can take prerequisites as electives, but in the hard technical courses, such as engineering, there are generally not enough elective hours available to include the accounting courses and the other courses you will need in order to make the change.

What Level of That Career Field Do You Want to Enter?

This is an important question for several reasons. The answer to this question may be by choice or by necessity. You may choose to go on to graduate school after you get your bachelor's degree but may not be able to do that for financial reasons. With the proper strategy, you can factor that into your career equation. Go ahead and enter the workforce, and then, when the opportunity presents itself, go on to grad school at night. Believe me, you will not be the first to take this route. The level you ultimately choose for your education will likely be a limiting factor in your career.

In What Location Do You Want to Go to School?

The answer to this question may be open or self-limiting. If you have plenty of money and a great GPA, it's probably a superfluous question, but most of us are not in this situation. First, not all colleges offer all disciplines. Your choice of discipline may be a determining factor. In other words, if that lovely, ivy-covered college sitting on the river only offers a liberal arts education and you want engineering, it's obviously not a match. Although this is pretty obvious, what is not so obvious is the limitation of a location once you are in the workforce. By this I mean if you live in Tucson, Arizona and want to get your graduate degree from Stetson University in Florida at night, you've got a problem. Your college locations are limited by: 1) Money, 2) Your GPA, 3) Where you live if you want part-time schooling. The point being, to the best of your ability, select your college, don't let exigencies select it for you.

What Particular School Do You Want to Attend?

You may want to go to Harvard or MIT or Stanford or some other highly rated school (who doesn't?) but that option may not be realistic. If you are in high school, you likely have more flexibility in the choice of schools than if you are in your undergraduate program. If you are independently wealthy and will be a legacy to MIT or Harvard, you can stop reading here and go on to the next section. Otherwise choose the best college that will take you, at any level. It does make a difference to your career.

Do You Want to Go to School Full-Time, Part-Time, Day, Night, Correspondence, Via E-Learning?

Ideally, you will probably want to go to the school of your choice, have your education paid for, attend classes during the day, and have an extensive social life at night. I read a book like that a long time ago, and that was the closest I ever came to this option. If you're like the rest of us, you will need some other combination of options. An alternative option is to work and go to school part-time. This is a real viable option, and it's done by a lot of people every day. It requires determination and severely impacts your social life. If you go to school full-time, you will probably go in the daytime. If you go to school part-time, it's probably because you are working, and you will probably have class at night. Some will take a night job just so they can go to school during the day. Correspondence courses are another viable option, but these are generally limited to undergraduate courses and very specific parts of graduate curricula. An extension of correspondence courses is the "distance learning" approach where you do most of your work through correspondence and then attend seminars at the university, usually in the summer. This is a great option, but it is limited in its career field offerings.

In the last few years, e-learning has come to the fore. This is a great approach even if you are working full-time and traveling. You can take a sack full of books and your laptop, and have some productive time at the airport waiting for the next plane or on the a long flight. Again, this approach is somewhat limited, and this approach may also be conducted in the same way as the extended campus option. This option will take a lot of planning and will eat into your social life, but so what? It's an option that's available, and if you choose to take it, go for it and good luck.

How Will You Pay for Your Schooling?

This is usually a grabber, at least for most of us. There are several options. First, you can have your education paid for by your family. That's wonderful.

Second, you can get a scholarship or a grant, several scholarships, or multiple grants. Good for you. This takes a lot of research and a lot of time answering questionnaires and interviewing, but otherwise is a good deal.

Third, you can take out student loans. Student loans are generally offered by financial institutions and backed by the federal government. Education loans are offered at very low interest rates.

Fourth, you can join the military and take advantage of their educational program. At one time, military personnel qualified for the so-called "GI Bill." But that specific instrument has been replaced with the military educational program. This is basically a matching annuity. A very good option. If you have taken the SATs and then the military entrance exams, you will likely show very well. If your scores are high enough, the military will send you to one of their schools that you choose. That's a great start on vectoring your field of work, and you can take correspondence or even some residence courses while you are in the service. Needless to say, you will have a service option of four or more years, but if you can get at least two years of college under your belt while you're in the service, you're way ahead of where you would be otherwise.

Fifth, some employers will pay or help pay for your education. A typical offering is for the employer to pay 75 percent of undergraduate tuition and 100 percent of graduate tuition. Paying for books, lab fees, and so on is up to you. This is a terrific way to get a degree but it takes a lot of grit to work all day and go to school at night. Besides that, you may be starting a family at the same time. This is a good place to put your scheduling skills to work.

Finally, you can work your way through college. That's a tough option, but it's done every day. Working takes its toll on homework and certainly on social life but in the long run it's definitely worth it. You must understand that, if you intend to work your way through, it will likely limit the schools you can attend and the way you do it. Chances are that you'll need to take the first two years at a community college while living at home and the last two years at a state university. If you are going to grad school under these conditions, you are likely working days and going to school at night. It works, but it requires drive and determination.

There are dozens of colleges and universities in the United States and dozens of colleges and universities internationally offering graduate-level project management degree programs and certificates. As you might imagine, the offerings are a conglomeration of just about every combination of on-campus, off-campus, Internet, degree, certificate combination you can think of. They are so complex that I can only generalize about these offerings. I organize these colleges and universities into five groups:

1. Colleges and universities that offer traditional, on-campus, graduate degree programs in project management
2. Colleges and universities that offer traditional, on-campus, graduate degree programs in business administration with a specialization in project management

3. Colleges and universities that offer traditional, on-campus, graduate degree programs in technical disciplines with options in project management
4. Colleges and universities that offer, off-campus, one or more of the above graduate degree programs through the Internet
5. Colleges and universities that offer certificate programs in project management, either on-campus or through the Internet

It is interesting to note that some colleges and universities recognize the PMP from the PMI. In the cases I have investigated, the PMP has a value of nine graduate-level hours counting toward a graduate degree. A graduate degree in project management usually consists of thirty-two hours of work.

To say it once again, the field of project management is changing rapidly. So is the support offered by colleges and universities. The best way I know of to find a consolidated listing of universities that provide support to these programs is to go to the PMI Web site at http://www.pmi.org/. Then, go to the "Professional Development and Careers" menu. Select "Academic Degree Accreditation." You can access the information there and then go to the Web site of the college or university of interest. You can search each school individually and determine which categories each offers. Then you can select the school that is most appropriate for your needs.

As an alternative, you can do an Internet search on colleges and universities, but you'll have to wade through a lot of inappropriate colleges. Also, you can do a search on "master of project management" or "master of science in project management."

At this point, you may be asking yourself: What role does a graduate degree in project management play in all this? This question is a little bit difficult to answer. Generally speaking, the project management curriculum covers the project management subject areas equivalent to those required for an expert project. In addition, there will be other courses required. Colleges and universities have little consistency of curricula other than for the core courses.

There are some other nuances that should be discussed at this point though. The first question back to you is: What do you intend to do with your career? The answer to that question is the real reason I divided the colleges and universities into the five categories.

If you want to go into project management as a long-term goal, you should select a program and university that results in a graduate degree in project management. The master of project management usually fills this ideal. Let's call this Category A.

If you want to add project management to your repertoire, but ultimately want to become a general manager or CEO or the like, you should choose an MBA program with a specialty in project management. Call this Category B.

If you are a technical person and want to have the ability to lead projects and be a functional manager also, you should select a program that adds project management to your technical core. Usually the master of science in project management will fill this requirement. We'll call this Category C.

As you can see, each of these areas follows a little different line of education. While the core courses are similar, the supporting courses and electives are quite different. Ergo, you should be careful to select the degree type that will give you the greatest return.

Let's refer to the five groups I talked about earlier and match them with the categories we just discussed.

1. Colleges and universities that offer traditional, on-campus, graduate degree programs in project management. These are Category A programs.
2. Colleges and universities that offer traditional, on-campus, graduate degree programs in business administration with a specialization in project management. These are Category B programs.
3. Colleges and universities that offer traditional, on-campus, graduate degree programs in technical disciplines with options in project management. These are Category C programs.
4. Colleges and universities that offer one or more of the above graduate degree programs through the Internet. These can be Category A, B, or C programs.
5. Colleges and universities that offer certificate programs in project management, either on-campus or through the Internet. As I said before, certificates are not degrees, and the programs that culminate in certificates are training programs, not educational programs. We'll go into these programs in just a moment.

What if you already have a graduate degree in another field, or don't want to go back and get another graduate degree or a doctorate at this time? The answer here could lie in getting a diploma, a certificate, or a certification in project management and add that to your credentials. These credentials actually fall into the category of training, which follows.

Expanding Your Training

You can expand your training with books and with seminars provided by private companies and colleges and universities. This is the time when you need to look back on the self-assessment tables earlier in this chapter. Where are your shortcomings? What areas do you need or want to improve? The answers to these questions will be different for each individual. At this point, I suggest you look back at the subject areas you need to improve and then look at the seminar and book listings provided by the AMA and the PMI for those areas. You can find these as follows:

AMA Books: http://www.amacombooks.org
AMA Seminars: http://www.amanet.org/seminars/index.htm
PMI Books: http://www.pmibookstore.org/
Search by keyword.

PMI Seminars:
Traditional: http://www.pmi.org/info/PDC_SW_Home.asp?nav=0402
E-Seminars: http://www.pmi.org/info/PDC_eSeminarsWorld.asp?nav=0404

Training, as we say in the workaday world, falls into two categories: in-house and out-of-house. In-house training is further categorized as internal training and referred training.

Internal training covers those training courses provided by your company training department as standard fare throughout the year. Courses that fall into this category are such things as: Introduction to Whatever, Ethics at Our Company, What Is Expected of You, Waste, Fraud, and Abuse, Sexual Harassment, and Socially and Politically Correct courses. Don't laugh. In a big company, you need to know what the expectations are, even if you don't agree with them. This is the way the company does business, and this is the baseline you are expected to follow. Also in this category are special training courses offered by outside vendors or consultants brought into the company. Usually these courses are quite specific and are generally pointed at specific disciplines. Many times, outside consultants will be invited to present technical or "human" courses that are of great value to managers. Examples of these kinds of courses are self-assessment courses for personality type, thinking type, management type, leadership type, and so on. These types of courses are extremely useful to you as a project manager, and my suggestion is to avail yourself of every one of these courses you can get. I know, when you are down in the trenches throwing back grenades and the personnel rep comes along and says your boss wants you to attend a course in social correctness next week, what your first response is likely to be. Let's say you're a little less than overjoyed. Don't reject it out of hand though. Hold your commitment or rejection until you've had an opportunity to assess this opportunity in the context of your overall strategy. Consider that this may be an opportunity to turn the reins of the project over to the person you have been mentoring to take your place. You have been mentoring someone to take your place, haven't you?

Out-of-house courses are courses offered by vendors, consultants, and companies that conduct their courses at locations other than on your campus. Most big seminars are offered this way because it is the most efficient way to conduct this kind of course. These courses run the gamut. Insofar as the company is concerned, these courses fall into one of two classes: known and unknown. The known courses are those that the company has sent people to before. The company knows the value of these courses and usually has no compunction about sending its employees to them. The unknown courses are those that have not yet been evaluated by the company (probably the training department), and the company may be reluctant to send you to one of these courses without more consideration. Outside courses and seminars cost between $500 and $2,000 per day per person, exclusive of travel, subsistence, and salary. With these kinds of numbers you can understand why the company wants to know why it's making this investment. If you find a course in this category that you feel is absolutely essential to your career, collect all the data you can and turn it over to your boss. Have your boss assess the value and take the findings to the training department. It will take a little longer but could be a real opportunity. Don't be too surprised if you get the answer that the training department has already evaluated the course because training departments usually have their "feelers" out for all kinds of related courses. As soon as the training companies find out your training department has a budget, they will be lined up at the door offering their wares. There are tons of training courses available. First, check with your training department to see the ones they have in inventory. You may be able to select some good ones from that list. Second, talk to your friends at other companies or look at the training course offerings recommended by the various project management organizations, particularly the one you are directly interested in. Finally, do a search on the Internet by "Project Management Training Courses" or by the specific area or course that you want. Also, look for project management training companies and see what they have to offer. These companies can provide whatever you want and a lot of things you never thought of.

Informal training is usually on-the-job training and is too diverse for discussion here.

Certification

The best place to look for certification is with the organization that is prevalent in your area or whose certification will be most beneficial to you. Who will this be? Will it be PMI? Will it be APM? Will it be some other organization? To get started in finding an organization for certification, first, select the organization that will best represent your interests from Figure 2-2. Remember too that a certificate may be the avenue you want to pursue. In this case check with your training department or do a search on the Internet. The numbers of certificate courses is immense.

Certificates and certifications have both intrinsic and extrinsic value. They have intrinsic value if they are satisfying to you. For instance, if you feel you must be certified as a project manager to satisfy your own needs and you accomplish that certification, then that satisfies an intrinsic need. They have extrinsic value, on the other hand, if they are satisfying to someone else. Let's say that certification is required by your job and you achieve that certification that satisfies an extrinsic need. Stated most succinctly, satisfaction of an intrinsic need gives you a good feeling, while satisfaction of an extrinsic need gives you money and position.

Each organization has specific areas that it insists on testing, and you must avail yourself of those areas. PMI is most rigorous in its treatment of knowledge areas. You must read their books and repeat their language and their terminology back to them. The other organizations are a bit more flexible in the terminology but are much broader in their performance and "attitude" testing and interviews. Refer to Chapter

2 to each of the certifying organizations for details regarding specific certifications. Refer to Chapter 6 for seminars that can offer certificates for attendance.

A certificate or certification indicates you have achieved a certain proscribed course of requirements. Most certainly that has meaning to some but the real question is: "Does it have meaning to your employer or potential employer in your specific business area?"

From a pragmatic point of view, make certain a certificate or certification has extrinsic and specific value before spending a lot of time and money on it. Certification is involved and expensive. As you saw above, in some cases it is valuable, and in other cases it is not so valuable.

Even though project management certification has been around for over twenty years, it is relatively new to industry. The primary reason, in my opinion, is that the purveyors of certification have been concentrating on the "supply side" of the curve and not the "demand side." Simply, this means they have concentrated on convincing individuals they needed certification but have not convinced industry to demand it. The secondary reason is that there is really no absolute standard. The PMI has tried diligently to establish a standard but has limited its certification process to knowledge. The other organizations use knowledge but rely heavily on practical experience, performance, attitude (persona), and interviews. Which is correct? It's a classic "Gown versus Town" (academic versus experience) argument. From my discussions with hiring authorities in industry, and from my own experience, I can say that performance is the most important factor in hiring and promoting project and program managers. Assuming that industry does accept certification as a requirement, which will it choose? Will it choose the knowledge-based PMP or the competency-based certifications like the aCPM3 or the IPMA Level B? So far, industry (I include the government in this discussion) has taken the traditional (and easy) way out and relied on performance. If, in the future, industry stipulates certification requirements, they will likely "escape between the horns of the dilemma" by only saying certification, rather than stipulating Certification A or Certification B. Just as soon as a company specifies one certification over another, it is putting itself in the position of value judge. Is a PMP more valuable than an aCPM1 or 2 (or vice versa)? If I were an officer in one organization and the certification of another organization was specified as a position requirement, I think I would want to know why. All I can say is, don't get caught up in the Gown versus Town argument just for the sake of argument.

I have been harping on performance as the prime criterion for hiring and promotion, and I won't budge from that position. But, what if you are a hiring manager and two candidates present with exactly the same performance qualifications, and one has a certification and the other does not? Which one will you choose? In that case, I believe the choice is obvious. You need to make the decision as to what the certification means to you and to your employer or potential employer.

Figure 7-6 shows that each organization has a different way of classifying their certifications: Level 1, Level C, Basic, and so on. Figure 7-6 presents the various levels and groups so they are more relatable. Use caution though because they are not absolute. In fact, in no way am I suggesting that if you know a particular skill set, you will be qualified to sit for the related certification. The purpose is to give you a general idea of how they relate to each other but not to provide an absolute comparison. If you need to understand exactly what is required for each certification, go to each organization of interest and read the detailed descriptions of their certification requirements.

Figure 7-6. Comparison of certifications and skill sets.

Organization	Certification	Comparative Skill Sets
AIPM	Project Director/Program Manager (Level 6)	Expert
	Project Manager (Level 5)	Advanced
	Project Team Member/Project Specialist (Level 4)	Basic
AMA	Project Management Certificate	Advanced
APM	Certificated International Project Manager (CIPM)	Specialist
	Senior Project Manager (Level 3)	Expert
	Certified Project Manager (Level 2)	Advanced
	Associate Project Management Professional (Level 1)	Basic
asapm	Senior management or project sponsor (SP)	Principal
	Resource Managers (RM)	Principal
	Project Office Manager (PO)	Expert
	Project Directors or Program Managers (P3)	Expert
	Project Managers (P2)	Advanced
	Project Specialists (P1)	Basic
	Project Team Members (TM)	Basic
IPMA	Certificated Projects Director (Level A)	Principal
	Certificated Projects Manager (Level B)	Expert
	Certificated Project Management Professional (Level C)	Advanced
	Certificated Project Management Practitioner (Level D)	Basic
JPMF	Project Management Architect (PMA)	Principal
	Project Manager Registered (PMR)	Advanced
	Project Management Specialist (PMS)	Basic
PMI	Project Management Professional (PMP)	Advanced
	Certified Associate in Project Management (CAPM)	Basic

CHAPTER 8

Improving Your Abilities

Perhaps you've read the recommended books and even attended the recommended seminars. This does not mean you are ready to lead a project or that your company will select you to lead any project other than projects requiring basic knowledge. You need experience.

Gaining Experience

If you were a high-wire walker in a circus, you would probably think it a good idea to gain your initial experience with a safety net you can fall into. Because of the importance of a project to a company, it is an equally good idea to have a "safety net." I recommend that you gain your initial project management experience under the tutelage of an experienced project manager, so that if you stumble, the impact to the project and to you will be minimized. As time goes on, however, you will gain more experience by taking on more responsibility and performing at a higher level.

Initial Experience

Initial experience will be gained by you as an associate or assistant project manager. It should be gained in some position that has a "safety net" to fall back on when you are confronted with a difficult situation. Only after you have gained initial experience, under supervised conditions, should you lead a project on your own.

You will gain experience from each and every assignment. But it is your task to ensure that the experience is positive and worthwhile. I remember that an associate once tried to justify the higher salary of a communications technician by saying: "He has twenty years' experience as a comm tech." My position was that he really has four years' experience, five times over. One can learn all he needs to know about this particular position in four years. After four years, he is welcome to stay in the same position if he wants to, but I'm not paying for it! What should that little quip mean to you? It should mean to keep your career onward and upward. Experience is a great thing, but it must be progressive experience.

Continuing Experience

Gain your experience at each level under the recommended conditions. For instance, the early levels recommend that you be an assistant or associate or at least under the tutelage of a senior project manager. Doing so is to your advantage. You get to pile up experience at a level but with a "backup" to go to if things start to sour. Even if everything is running smoothly, you get the opportunity to observe another project manager in action. Believe me, that's worth a lot.

As you read through the five levels you found that a period of experience was recommended for each level. These periods have been determined by research and personal experience. They assume you have achieved the knowledge requirements early in the period and that the experience was applying this knowledge. This requirement may or may not be what your employer or potential employer requires. Of course, the employer's requirement must take precedence. The idea presented in the experience requirements is to understand and apply your knowledge base at each level and ensure good (better yet, outstanding) performance. Then, don't dwell at that level. Move on to the next level.

You really want to look upon the experience recommendations as an advantage to you, not a disadvantage. Everyone gets excited and ready to jump on the next project, but from your standpoint as well as from the position of the company, you need to ensure that you are ready. You want your next position to be a challenge, not a struggle.

Developing Your Persona

"Mirror, mirror on the wall. . . ."[1] Don't we all wish we had such insight? Unfortunately, we will need to review our persona more traditionally. Your persona is the sum of all the things that go into your makeup—it's who you are. It's your personality, your attitude, your method of doing things, and how others perceive you.

Again, there are intrinsic factors and extrinsic factors. In this case, the intrinsic factors include your natural inclinations and attitude. Are you a "things" person or a "people" person? Are you the "steely-eyed captain of the ship'' or the ''happy-go-lucky co-pilot'' who takes it as it comes? You can change your natural inclinations and attitude, but not much.

Now, the extrinsic factors. These include your education, your training, and your experiences. Additionally, the impact your peers have on your thinking is tremendous. Extrinsic factors can be changed a lot. Every time you take a course or a seminar, you view things a little differently as a result of what you learned. But here too is where they come together. For instance, the experiences you bring into a seminar modulate what you take away from the seminar and what you will bring with you to the next seminar. Will the project manager sitting next to you take away exactly the same understanding? I don't think so. It is the sum of these intrinsic and extrinsic factors that makes you unique.

Whenever I think of persona, I think of a little story one of my graduate advisers used to tell. He said that every day at five o'clock the subways were filled with people heading to night classes to get their MBAs or some other degree. They were convinced that those degrees would make all the difference and that they would then be on their way to success. His position was that it may make a difference in some cases, but the problems the majority of them had were personality problems. That's what was holding them back. His position certainly backs up the old saw that says: ''The very strengths that got you here are the same ones that are keeping you from going any further.''

Assessing Your Persona

Take a look at your persona, both the intrinsic factors and the extrinsic factors, and find out what you think of yourself and what others think of you as well. If you don't care, now is a good time to stop reading! There are a number of ways to determine your personal and leadership characteristics. One of the best I know is: *Myers-Briggs Type Indicator (MBTI)*, an idea that was developed by Peter B. Myers and Katherine Briggs and made into a seminar. Instructors certified by Consulting Psychologists teach the seminar and evaluate the summary results.

The idea behind this course is that people have a primary style of operating that is expressed in four-letter factors that are parts of four pairs of factors. The factors are: Extroverted (E) versus introverted (I); sensing (S) versus intuition (N); thinking (T) versus feeling (F); and judging (J) versus perceiving (P). There are sixteen combinations, each reflecting a different personality type. The MBTI tends to reflect your intrinsic factors. As I said before, you can change these factors but not much. Over time, I have watched my MBTI go from I-N-T-J (INTJ) to E-S/N-T-J to E/I-S/N-T-J back to basically I-N-T-J. The shared characters (that is, E/I) are the result of scores being exactly the same in the two factors. My changes were due, in large part, to the positions I held at a particular moment in time. It seems to be sort of an application of *Situational Leadership* (SL)—you do what you have to do when you have to do it!

MBTI has been around a long time and has become the de facto personality test in industry. I believe in it so strongly that I had my son take the test, at my own expense, while he was still a freshman in college. I use MBTI, presented and evaluated by certified instructors, in all my team seminars.

Improving Your Abilities

As I said at the outset, leadership is the most important attribute of a project manager. There are dozens of leadership courses available as seminars and training courses and dozens of books on the subject as well. One of the best initial evaluation courses I have come across is *Leadership Practices Inventory (LPI)*. LPI is a test instrument designed to show your leadership practices. The LPI was created by James Kouzes and Barry Posner. It is a self- or local assessment tool that is clever in its construction. A self-assessment questionnaire is filled in by the leader (you). It is further filled in by up to ten peers, supervisors, and subordinates. Include as many different categories as possible. When the results are returned, they are transferred to a matrix sheet and evaluated. The matrix sheet decodes the questions, resulting in scores that evaluate your Challenging, Inspiring, Enabling, Modeling, and Encouraging leadership practices. It's a bit more involved than this but you get the idea.

I recommend that LPI be followed up by *Situational Leadership* (SL). SL is a seminar created by Paul Hersey and Ken Blanchard. It is taught by certified university associate instructors. The basis of the course is that different situations call for different leadership styles. They call the styles they teach: Delegating, Participating, Selling, and Telling. Which style you use depends how the task is delivered and the relationship between the leader and the followers. One style just won't work for all situations. This course has been around for a long time, and it is one of the best leadership courses I have seen.

I think you will find the relationship between the leadership styles of *Situational Leadership* (delegating, participating, and so on) similar to the people-to-people styles of *I'M OK, You're OK* (parent-to-child, adult-to-adult, and so on).

The group courses are best set up by the training department of your company, so that the "language" that is a part of each of these courses is common to all project managers and to other leaders in your company. This way, when someone says: "Oh, I know him, he's an INTJ," everyone will know what the speaker is talking about.

Suggested Seminars

Myers-Briggs Type Indicator (MBTI)
Consulting Psychologists Press, Inc.
3803 E. Bayshore Road
Palo Alto, CA 94303
Phone: 800 624-1765
Web site: www.mbti.com

Leadership Practices Inventory (LPI)
Instruction package available to training departments.
Pfeiffer & Company
8517 Production Avenue
San Diego, CA 92121
Phone: 619 578-5900
Fax: 619 578-2042
Web site: http://www.pfeiffer.com/
E-mail: customercare@Pfeiffer.com

Situational Leadership
The Center for Leadership Studies
230 West Third Avenue
Escondido, CA 92025-4180
Phone: 800 330-2840 or 760 741-6595
Fax : 760 747-9384
Web site: http://www.situational.com/#

Suggested Reading

Harris, Thomas. *I'm OK, You're OK*. New York: Avon, 1976.

Improving Your Performance

Performance is the quality level at which your experience is exhibited. It is reasonable to say that experience is time-related and performance is quality-related. For your own personal benefit, it is best if your performance is acknowledged by some official act by your supervisor or the enterprise or corporation. Recognition such as a "Letter of Commendation," "Team Leader of the Month," or "Project Manager of the Year" are the types I am talking about. Something concrete, objective, and portable! Without making a pest of yourself, try to get every major accomplishment recognized. Keep copies of each and every one of these awards and certificates.

Review Your Performance

The absolute worst reviewer of your performance is you! You will either be overly critical or will rationalize your performance. This is just human nature. (Perhaps I should have had this section titled "Have Your Performance Reviewed" rather than "Review Your Performance.") Nevertheless, you need to constantly keep a finger on your own pulse. It is essential that you understand how you are perceived by your peers, by your team members, by your management, and by your customers. At every occurrence, ask yourself: "Is this pulse reading I am taking now a constant or just a single reading"? You will not be perceived by everyone in the same way all the time. What you are striving for is a "best fit," a Root Mean Square (RMS) of all the evaluations of all the people in all the positions on all the projects you have interfaced with.

Enhance Your Performance

Once again, review the equation for project management success:

$$\text{Knowledge} + \text{Experience} + \text{Persona} \times \text{Performance} = \text{Success}$$

This means that you use all the knowledge you can gain as leverage, apply that knowledge to gain experience, and through your persona, show performance. This is the only path to project management success.

Back in Chapter 7, you went through an exercise of checking off and evaluating your abilities as they were required for each skill set. We are at a point now where you need to do the same thing for your performance. Unfortunately, I can't give you a checklist this time. What I suggest you do is list each project or program you have led. Inside that listing, like an outline, list the objectives that you had for each project. Then grade your performance against each goal. It's a good idea to have some of your associates work with you in remembering what the goals and objectives were. If you have not yet led a project, do the same thing for projects you have participated in. At this point, the objective is to establish a methodology rather than worrying about specifics.

From now on, make your list at the beginning of each project you participate in or lead. Evaluate your performance, and ask your peers to help you both with making the list and with the evaluation. Now you have a technique that's worthwhile. It's something to which you can point with pride.

What we have done is to establish a set of objectives that you grade at the completion of each as they occur. After just a short while, this technique will make you goal-oriented. You will know your precise performance from day to day. A trick I have found to be helpful is to have these goals and performance evaluations in a visible place. You may want to put them on a white board or on the flyleaf of your notebook. You may want to list the goal for today or for this week on the whiteboard and keep the others in another place. Frequently, an interesting thing happens. People notice the technique and commend you for it. Some of them start using the same technique. Your boss notices the goals you have posted in a visible place and sees your progress. This is a pretty good idea, isn't it?

Note

1. The evil queen questions her magic mirror in the Grimm brothers' fairy tale *Snow White and the Seven Dwarfs*.

PART IV

APPLYING YOUR SKILLS TO PROJECTS AND PROGRAMS

In Chapter 1 we talked about how the project management process can be used. We said that the process can be used by individuals in the performance of their individual tasks as well as by project leaders to lead the performance of the tasks of others.

In Chapter 4, we established the project and program types. We saw that there are seven types of projects and programs. Each project or program has its own characteristics, and as we progressed through the types, we saw that they tended to get larger and larger and more and more complex. We went from a small project consisting of perhaps a half-dozen people performing a relatively simple task to a large scale program consisting of hundreds of people and performing a complex set of tasks.

Clearly, one type of project manager with one set of learned tools cannot lead tasks of such breadth and diversity. This was resolved by introducing five project and program skill sets in Chapter 4.

Now is the time to put it all together. To apply the project skill levels to the project and program types. It's time to put the round peg into the round hole and the square peg into the square hole—so to speak.

In this chapter I hope to show how all that training you got in Chapter 4 is now applicable to the project and program tasks you are to lead.

CHAPTER 9

Matching the Skill Sets to Projects and Programs

Have you wondered what it's like to lead a project or program? It can be fun; it can be exciting; it can be educational. Or, it can be challenging; it can be difficult; it can be nerve-wracking. Chances are, it will be some combination of all these things. How the project runs and ends will, in large part, depend on you and how well you used the "knowledge leverage" you gained as a result of Part II.

Throughout Part II, we talked about the different levels of proficiency necessary to lead different project and program levels. Now we can talk about the projects and programs where you will apply that knowledge. For starters, Figure 9-1 is a cross-reference between Proj-

Figure 9-1. Skill sets as they apply to project and program categories.

Project/Program Category	Skill Set
Small Project	Basic
Intermediate Project	Advanced
Large Project	Advanced
Program	Expert
Virtual Project or Program	Specialty
International Program	Specialty
Large-Scale (Grand) Program	Principal

ect/Program Category and Skill Set. The reason there are seven categories and only five skill sets is that the difference between intermediate projects and large projects is principally size and can be overcome by experience. The difference between virtual programs and international programs is that they are both specialties, not unlike pharmaceuticals being a specialty and aerospace being a specialty. However, once you step over the specialty line the options are enormous. It is not possible or even advisable to list all the specialty skills necessary to serve all the programs, so I have simply combined them into a "Specialty" category skill set.

Many of the characteristics of the project and program types are similar, but there are some characteristics that distinguish one from the other. I have enumerated nineteen factors that characterize the different project and program types. Figure 9-2 lists the factors in the left column and defines them for use by all levels in the right column. Note that the required skill set is the last row in the table.

From here on, we will be generalizing about project types rather than referring to specific projects. What we want to do is to separate the project types using some discriminators so you will have an idea of what different project levels are all about.

To avoid redundancy, I will present only the characteristics that distinguish one stage from another. Additional information will be provided as necessary.

A Small Project

A small project is the most basic of projects and is the workhorse of the project management system. There are numerically more small projects than all the other project types put together. For all practical purposes, a small project is an order rather than a project—that is, a task order assigned to a project "manager" to get the work done. The project manager does not "own" the people on the project, but rather they belong to the functional managers and are simply "loaned" to the project as necessary. Neither does the project manager have the authority to move resources to accomplish the task. Many times, the people working on the small project will change from day to day. This is the epitome of the matrix system and gives the company tremendous latitude in handling its people but can be a real headache for the project manager.

A small project requires the project manager (coordinator) be knowledgeable of and able to apply at least the Basic Skill Set

(text continues on page 116)

Figure 9-2. Characteristics of projects and programs.

Tasks:	Enumerates the kinds of tasks you might expect to find in a particular level. There is considerable overlap and sometimes the only difference that separates one project type for another is value or complexity.
Customer:	Defines the customer type you would expect to find in each category. Every project or program is performed for a customer. The customer may be in the same operating unit as you, in the same division, in the same company, in a different company, or in a different organization. Who the customer is will have a huge bearing on how the project or program is conducted and "sold off."
Value:	Dollars are used as the common denominator for consistency. In reality, the smaller projects are not evaluated or conducted on dollar value. Instead, they are controlled by schedule and labor hours used to complete the project.
Duration:	Time is used as the common denominator for consistency. Greater technical or programmatic complexity will result in longer project duration.
Risk Level:	Every project has risk. Risk is one of the major factors for categorizing projects into different levels. Generally, the greater the project risk, the higher the level of classification of the project.
Complexity*:	Projects contain technical complexity and programmatic complexity. Technical complexity can result from pushing the state of the art, and so on.

(continues)

Figure 9-2. (Continued).

	Programmatic complexity can result from the need to make alliances, or the location of contributors, and so on.
Contract Type(s):	Contracts have base types and fee (profit) provisions used in combination. The most rigid is Firm Fixed Price (FFP) and is generally used on programs that can be well defined. The most forgiving is Cost Plus Fixed Fee (CPFF) and is generally used on programs that cannot be well defined. Other combinations involve applying award fee (AF) provisions and incentive fee (IF) provisions to the base contract types such as Fixed Price (FP) and Cost Plus (CP), and so on. You can look upon the award and incentive factors as bonuses.
No. of People:**	The number of people assigned to a project, on average. Some persons will be assigned to the project for the full duration and others for shorter periods.
Disciplines†:	The crafts or specialties required to perform the task.
Schedule Tools:	Schedule tools are those tools used to present and maintain the timeline for the project. Schedule tools vary from handwritten, indentured lists to highly sophisticated software applications that interface with all the operating functions of the project, including the accounting system. Schedule tools should be selected to provide the level of support needed for the project. Not too sophisticated and not too simple.

Accounting Base:	The base used to collect and account for costs. The simplest is time cards or time sheets for labor and invoices for materials. The most sophisticated is methods that input directly to the accounting system with little or no human intervention.
Accounting Tools:	The tools used to account for budget and expenditures. Accounting tools vary from pencil and paper to sophisticated software applications. It is common for companies to have their own accounting tools based on the way they do business.
Organization Type:	The two basic types of organizations that support projects are matrix and projectized. In the matrix method people are assigned to a functional organization and allocated to a project for some period of time or to accomplish some task. In the projectized method, the people are assigned full-time to the project.
PM Reports to:	The person to whom the project manager reports for a particular type or level of project. Usually the PM reports to a line manager or director or to a PMO manager or director. In some cases, the PM reports administratively to a line manager and technically to a PMO.
Materials and Subcontracts:	The office responsible for identifying, procuring, accounting for, and verifying applicability and existence of materials and subcontracts for this specific project level or type.

(continues)

Figure 9-2. (Continued).

Quality:	The source of the quality function for this specific project level or type.
Effectiveness:	The category of effectiveness usually includes combinations of Reliability, Availability, Maintainability (RAM), Human Engineering (Ergonomics), Configuration Management, and Safety
Facilities and Equipment‡:	The responsibility for defining and providing facilities and equipment for this specific project level or type.
Team Training:	The level of team training required for this specific project level or type.
Applicable Skill Set:	The skill set (see Chapter 5) a project manager needs to prosecute this type or level of project.

*Complexity drives cost/price/value, project duration, and usually risk. Additionally, on a program, complexity may drive contract type. Gathering the definitions of Risk Level and Complexity together results in understanding that these factors have a great bearing on the level of a project.
**The number of people assigned to a project or program generally indicates its complexity. The complexity can be technical or programmatic or both. A small number of people generally indicates a low complexity; a great number of people generally indicates high complexity. There are exceptions. Usually, the greater the number of people, the higher the cost.
†A small number of disciplines generally indicates low project programmatic complexity; a great number of disciplines generally indicates a high project complexity, either programmatic or technical or both. A greater number of disciplines generally indicates a higher cost.
‡Facilities and equipment are capital items and are usually paid for and accounted for by the company. In some cases equipment may be provided by the customer as Customer Furnished Equipment (CFE) or Government Furnished Equipment (GFE), and facilities may be provided by the customer outright or leased for a specific program.

(Chapter 4), meaning subject areas 1 through 7, in detail and the remaining subject areas at a lesser level.

Figure 9-3 shows the characteristics of a small project. You can compare this table to the tables presented for the other project and program types and see where the differences lie at a glance.

Figure 9-3. Small project characteristics.

Tasks:	Installation, small software projects, small R&D projects, administrative projects.
Customer:	The customer is inside the company, and may be in the same or a different operating unit.
Value:	Usually less than $500,000 total.
Duration:	Usually 1 month to 6 months.
Risk Level:	Low.
Complexity:	Low.
Contract Type(s):	No contract.
Number of People:	Usually 5 or fewer.
Disciplines:	Same or closely related.
Schedule Tools:	Simple—Indentured list or bar chart.
Accounting Base:	Labor hours.
Accounting Tools:	Time cards/sheets.
Organization Type:	Matrix.
PM Reports to:	Line manager.
Materials and Subcontracts:	Identified by a management team, procured and accounted for by Materiel Department, verified by project.
Quality:	Ad hoc.
Effectiveness:	Ad hoc.
Facilities and Equipment:	Identified by management team, provided by the company.
Team Training:	Minimal.
Applicable Skill Set:	Basic

Now that we have seen the overall characteristics of the small project, we can parse the project into the stages described in Chapter 1.

Initiate Stage

The management staff of your group usually initiates a small project. Once the project has been defined in terms of its requirements, it will be assigned to you for implementation. In this case, the management staff is the customer.

Planning Stage

The Planning Stage is only a few days at most. Your input requirements consist of some written requirements and likely some verbal direction.

You will generate an abbreviated Project Plan. The schedule will have a start date and a completion date and show intermediate events as line items. The budget will be in labor hours per reporting period and be a sum of the period hours of the individual periods. The budget also contains the labor hours of others to be used in the task. These hours are stipulated in the budget as specific, additional hours and in the schedule as subtasks with start and complete dates or performance periods. After you have completed the Project Plan, you should have the person issuing the task approve it.

At this point, you need to assemble your team to establish that each person knows what his or her role in the overall task is. Simply discussing the role each person plays usually suffices for team training for a project at this level, but may disclose some interesting disconnects. Therefore, you need to have this meeting.

Kickoff is a technicality but nevertheless a real point in the project. Your Kickoff occurs when the Project Plan is approved.

Execution Stage

The content of the Execution Stage is determined by the needs of the project as expressed in the task statement and documented in the Project Plan. For a small project, it is likely that you will lead the technical team as well as be the project manager.

The design phase of small projects is usually abbreviated and consists of product details, performance, and final test. Usually for this size project, the design phase consists not of equipment design, but of simple tasks such as listing pin outs and load lists for installation tasks.

For small R&D tasks, the origin of the need and all prior work is reviewed and the protocol of the period is determined.

The materiel department normally purchases the items required and then provides these items to the project. The departments may or may not assign a specific person to the task depending on the size and importance of the task.

The Execution Stage is where the entire physical task is accomplished. As stated in the table, installation tasks, small software projects, small R&D tasks, and administrative tasks as well as numerous other similar tasks are performed as small projects. The Execution Stage ends with the Test Period.

The purpose of the Test Period is to confirm that the product meets the requirements. This may mean a physical test in the case of a hardware or software project, but for small R&D projects or an administrative project it may mean an inventory of the results.

Closure Stage

The Closure Stage for a small project is simple but still needs to be done. Ensure your customer is satisfied with the completed task. Satisfaction must relate to the scope agreed upon.

Perform whatever handover process is necessary such as signing release papers. Write a simple "Lessons Learned" paper even if this project was the same as others.

The people were not directly assigned to your project, so you don't need to be concerned about finding jobs for them. However, it is a good idea to visit the people that supported you in this project and thank them; even an e-mail will suffice. It will make it a lot easier to get their support the next time. Most organizations have some performance review system for evaluating how raises and promotions are distributed. I suggest you make notes on each contributor's performance during the performance of the project. You may be asked for inputs to individual performance reports at a later date, and you'll be glad you made the notes. Further, it will give you insight into individual performance when the next project comes along. A little effort now saves a lot of head scratching and confusion later.

As you can see, the small task using the project management process is quite simple. But don't equate simplicity with importance; your task is very important to the overall success of your department and your company. While the process may be simple, performance may or may not be simple. Performing under these conditions will try your leadership skills, abilities, and patience.

An Intermediate Project

There are important differences between a small project and an intermediate project. The primary differences lie in the assignment of people and in the complexity and risk of the project. For an intermediate project, people are assigned to the project for performance of the work you define although you may still be required to "share" some team members with another project. But while a team member is assigned to your project, their performance is your responsibility and under your authority. You will find that the complexity of an intermediate project is greater than that of a small project, and with increased complexity usually comes increased risk. So, Risk Management (20) should be high on the list of subject areas you have your arms around.

At this level, projects are more complex and more subject to change. Here is where you will apply your knowledge of Change Control (12) for the project and Configuration Management (15) for the product.

An intermediate project requires the project manager to be knowledgeable of at least the Advanced Skill Set. In the following paragraphs you will see why. You are required to use all twenty-four of the subject areas for this project and will likely be confronted with Negotiation (40) demands and could be required to use other subject areas as well.

Figure 9-4 shows the characteristics of an intermediate-level project. Comparing this table to the tables presented for the other project and program types, you can see where the differences lie at a glance.

Now that we have seen the overall characteristics of the intermediate-level project we can parse the project into the stages described in Chapter 1.

Initiate Stage

An intermediate-level project is usually initiated by your group management in response to their own needs or the needs of another group in the company. Once the project has been defined in terms of its requirements, it will be assigned to you for implementation. The requestor or the requesting group is the customer.

Planning Stage

Your Planning Stage starts at the time of project assignment. In this case, your project plan is relatively simple but must include all the ele-

Figure 9-4. Intermediate project characteristics.

Tasks:	Installation, construction, administrative, medium R&D, subsystem, small system.
Customer:	The customer is inside the company and may be in the same or a different operating unit.
Value:	Usually between $500,000 and $1,000,000.
Duration:	Usually 6 months to 18 months.
Risk Level:	Low to moderate.
Complexity:	Installation, construction, administrative, medium R&D, subsystem, small system.
Contract Type(s):	The customer is inside the company and may be in the same or a different operating unit.
Number of People:	Usually between $500,000 and $1,000,000.
Disciplines:	Usually 6 months to 18 months.
Schedule Tools:	Low to moderate.
Accounting Base:	Labor hours, materials invoices.
Accounting Tools:	Time cards/sheets, invoices.
Organization Type:	Matrix.
PM Reports to:	Line manager.
Materials and Subcontracts:	Identified by a management team, procured and accounted for by Materiel Department, verified by project.
Quality:	Ad hoc.
Effectiveness:	Ad hoc.
Facilities and Equipment:	Identified by project, provided by the company.
Team Training:	1 day.
Applicable Skill Set:	Advanced

ments necessary for a complete project plan. The best plans are those that have participation of team members so they can "buy in" to the conduct of the project. Explaining the needs will put demands on your Communication (10) skills and your Information Management (13) techniques.

Even though the materiel department is responsible for providing materials, you are responsible for overall schedule. This conundrum is typical of these kinds of projects.

For these projects, you need to negotiate for the people who will support your project. Likely you will have to negotiate hard because it is a provider's market, and all the other project managers want the best people they can get too. You may need to get "up to speed" in Negotiation (40) in a hurry. You should have Quality (21) involved in all these interfaces.

Once assignments have been made and the project plan completed, call the people together for a team training session. This situation will test your knowledge and application of the Training (24) subject area. The training session does not need to be a fancy "dog and pony show" but it must turn the group (or as we used to say, "a column of mobs") into a team. A team is a group of people working together for a cause higher than their own individual needs.

As the leader of the team, you need to be prepared to start the session off on the right foot. This will test not only your Training (24) abilities, but also your Meeting and Negotiation Skills. The first thing on the training agenda should be the objective of the team. Next, give your team the schedule and any important milestones. Then, your presentation should include the organization—the hierarchy, if you will. The breadth and depth of the organization will vary in accordance with the complexity of the task. If it is not obvious, the charter of each element may also be presented, but don't tell them their jobs. If they already know them, treat them as professionals, if they don't know their jobs, send them back to their functional managers. Finally, have each project element stand up and specify the input products they need to do their jobs, who they expect to provide these products, and when.

Document this effort and have each team member sign the input and output sheets that apply to them. Each team member gets a copy of their sheets, and you get copies of all of them. Hopefully, you never need to have a session where you must refer to the sheets. Just going through this process will instill your seriousness in their minds. Besides, if you don't have these understandings and you have to resolve these interface issues every day, you'll never get the rest of your job done.

You will likely know what each job is, and after you set up these sessions for a few projects, know them by heart. Your people will be "chomping at the bit" to get on with the job, but make sure they complete the team session first. Remember, just as soon as the job starts, they will be spending your money and consuming your schedule and contributing to your reputation. Make sure everyone understands all the objectives of the training sessions, then get on with it.

Kickoff for these projects can be accomplished shortly after the team session and lasts about half of a day. It is always a good idea to have each group stand up and go through their responsibilities and their schedules.

Execution Stage

The Execution Stage is what the project is designed for as far as management and the customer are concerned. You've planned your project and trained the team, now is the time to make it work.

At the intermediate level, projects become not only complex but diverse as well. As you saw in Figure 9-4, these projects cover the waterfront. You may or may not have a design phase, but if you do, it is likely you will use a rapid prototype of both the hardware and the software. It is not at all unusual for a project at this level to have several components being addressed simultaneously. For instance, if you have an IT project that requires facility modifications to make room for the final configuration, you will have software and hardware design or prototyping going on at the same time as the physical work of modifying the facility. It will require that you be in several places at one time.

Procurements will "fall out" at several levels and at several times, and control of the situation will tax your understanding of Procurement and Contracts (17). The most important procurements are the so-called long-lead items. These are items that require a long time to produce or are in such demand you have to wait a long time for them. Whatever the reason, they can bring your project to a screeching halt if not ordered in time to get them when and where they are needed. Usually these are subcontracts and either create new products or heavily modify existing products.

The design process will reveal the next series of procurements. The details of each really won't be known until they are revealed by design need. The final level is the common items that can be purchased "off-the-shelf." Scheduling the delivery of all procured products is critical because they pace the critical path of your implementation and integration activity. Remember: "For want of the nail the shoe was lost; For want of the shoe the horse was lost; For want of the horse the rider was lost; For want of the rider the battle was lost; For want of the battle the kingdom was lost; And all for the want of a horse shoe nail."[1] Criticality was understood even in Ben Franklin's day.

In this case, implementation will consist of bringing all the elements together into a single system.

Testing will be incremental and consists of compiling the unit tests of each element of the system, the results of subsystem tests, and the results of the final system test. This process is common to all the activities at this level of projects, even construction and administrative projects.

Final testing will draw the entire system together. If there are discrepancies, they must be captured in Discrepancy Reports (DRs) and dispositioned as Action Items (AIs) for closure. Performance errors must be fixed and the final test rerun in its entirety. Whenever all the AIs have been closed, the system should be accepted. Knowing this, you will have run the final test a number of times before the customer arrives just to make sure the system runs properly during the real final test.

Closure Stage

The Closure Stage will have begun at final test and the ensuing AIs will have been captured. Final Test is usually a part of the Closure Stage to ensure that the final AIs are closed to the customer's satisfaction. Then it's time for handover, the Final Report, and the "Lessons Learned" paper.

Wrap up the project by having the customer sign off acceptance of the system. No matter what your internal procedures are, it is a good idea to have the customer sign off. We said at the outset that a project has a beginning and an end. This is the time for the end. If there is no acceptance that the project is completed, little items could bug you for a long time. Likely you will be graded on the project, and if it never ends, you never get the grade and the recognition you deserve.

Finally, write a Final Report that summarizes the project. The Final Report usually goes to the customer and is filed internally. Additionally, you should write a "Lessons Learned" paper. This paper is an internal document and should not go to the customer. Hopefully, it will be a short paper and should reflect the changes that were made or that need to be made to processes and procedures for future projects. This is a good reference for you and may prove valuable to other project managers who run similar projects.

A Manpower Plan is part of your Project Plan and shows how people are phased into and out of the project. This plan is kept up-to-date to allow the functional managers to adjust their personnel availability for other projects. Even though a project has a beginning and an end, the people are phased in and phased out. To have them all available on day one and to let them all go after the final test would be a disaster. You should be "shedding" people and allowing them to go back to their functional managers all along. Hopefully, at this point, you only have yourself and the senior technical lead left (if you had one at all).

Writing thank-you notes to all who participated in your project is a good idea. If you can get some simple "give-aways" from marketing or sales, the task is that much easier.

A Large Project

The differences between an intermediate project and a large project are due primarily to size. But, large projects are an inherent part of a company's planning and contribute to its overall financial performance. Because of this, your Project Plan must establish Project Success Criteria (8) and a Strategy (9) that ensures success. The size and complexity of large projects puts demands on your knowledge of Structure (14) and Life Cycle (16).

In Chapter 4 you saw that a large project requires the project manager to be knowledgeable of at least the Advanced Skill Set. You are required to use all twenty-four of the subject areas for this project plus, of course, the earlier areas and a knowledge of all the other areas, to a lesser degree. The size and complexity changes lead directly to increased risk and thus more complex Risk Management (20).

Figure 9-5 shows the characteristics of a large project. Comparing this table with the tables presented for the other project and program types, you can see where the differences lie at just a glance.

Initiate Stage

Initiation of a large project usually begins with an idea by management that a certain task should be accomplished. That task is then passed on

Figure 9-5. Large project characteristics.

Tasks:	Installation, construction, administrative, medium to large R&D, subsystem, medium system.
Customer:	The customer is inside the company and is usually in a different operating unit.
Value:	Usually greater than $1,000,000.
Duration:	Usually more than 1 year.
Risk Level:	Moderate.
Complexity:	Moderate.
Contract Type(s):	No contract.
Number of People:	Usually more than 10.
Disciplines:	Usually multidisciplinary.
Schedule Tools:	Charts, software applications.
Accounting Base:	Labor hours, materials invoices.
Accounting Tools:	Time cards/sheets, invoices.
Organization Type:	Matrix.
PM Reports to:	Group leader.
Materials and Subcontracts:	Identified by a management team, procured and accounted for by Materiel Department, verified by project.
Quality:	Ad hoc or assigned depending on size and complexity.
Effectiveness:	RMA and/or other.
Facilities and Equipment:	Identified by project, provided by the company.
Team Training:	1-2 days.
Applicable Skill Set:	Advanced

to a committee or group to do the initial planning and justify the need. The output of this group, once approved, becomes the requirements document for the project. A group leader is usually appointed, and this person (or persons) becomes "the customer." Once the project has been defined in terms of its requirements, it is assigned to you for implementation. Now is a good time to consult previous "Lessons Learned" papers for hints concerning pitfalls or shortcuts that did or did not work on similar projects in the past. If a mentor is available, discuss any concerns you've encountered or anticipate.

Planning Stage

The Planning Stage starts when the project is assigned to you. A large project includes many tasks, so your project plan must include all the elements necessary for a complete project plan. In a large project, Resource Management (11) drives the Project Plan, and you need to concentrate on that subject area. Resource Management will, in turn, drive how you organize (19).

In the case of the large project, you advertise for, evaluate, award, manage, and receive the materials and subcontracts associated with the project. This can be a large job and is frequently accomplished by one or two persons. One person handles the purchases of standard off-the-shelf equipment and software and another person handles all the subcontracts. The size and complexity of the task determines whether you have one or two people performing this task and whether they are assigned as full- or part-timers. When you start purchasing materials and subcontracts within the project, your job increases significantly. Typically, the technical departments (such as engineering) define the materials and subcontracts necessary and must initiate the specifications for these items. You, the program officer, are responsible for the "Statement of Work" that accompanies the specification, and the subcontracts administrator or manager handles the terms and conditions (Ts & Cs) and the whole procurement package. Subcontracts can make or break a project, and at this level, you must thoroughly understand "Procurements & Subcontracts (17)." Even if you have a subcontracts manager, it will be necessary to manage (not micromanage) this process from the top down.

This is a large project, so you need to Negotiate (40) for the people who will support your project.

Once assignments have been made, call the people together for a training session. This action will test your knowledge and application of subject area Training (24). The training session must turn the group into a team. Use the training session for Team Building (23) to accomplish this.

As leader of the team, you need to start the session off on the right foot. Once again, the first thing on the training agenda should be the objective of the team. Next, give team members the schedule and any important milestones. Then, your presentation should include the organization. The breadth and depth of the organization will vary in accordance with the complexity of the task. As before, have each project element stand up and specify the input products they need to do their jobs, who they expect to provide them, and when. Document the effort and have each team member sign the input and output sheets that apply to them. Each team member gets a copy of their sheets, and you get copies of all of them. I keep harping on this point for a reason. It is the heart and soul of getting your project job done. You can't, and shouldn't, do it alone. Every member of the team must be a contributor, and they must all act together as a team. Drive this point home, and then get on with it.

Kickoff for these projects can be accomplished shortly after the team session and will last about a half of a day. It is always a good idea to have each group stand up and go through their responsibilities and their schedules. For large projects, it is usually a good idea to invite management to the kickoff to show you know what you are doing. Obviously, you will want to have several "dry runs" beforehand to ensure that everything goes well.

Execution Stage

The Execution Stage is what the project is designed for as far as management and the customer are concerned. You've planned your project and trained the team, now is the time to make it work.

As you saw in Figure 9-5, these projects may appear to be similar to intermediate projects but they are larger and more complex. To keep up with the complexity of all of these "goings on," it is a good idea to employ an Earned Value Management System (18) to understand exactly where you are in terms of accomplishment.

With a project of this size, if it is for hardware or software, it is likely you will have a design. You will likely have a pure design portion and a rapid prototype portion for both hardware and software. It is not at all unusual for a project at this level to have several components being addressed simultaneously. For instance, if you have a project that uses off-the-shelf hardware and software in conjunction with new hardware and software, it will require you to be in several places at one time and changing hats frequently.

As with intermediate projects, procurements will "fall out" at several levels and at several times. The design process will reveal the next level of procurements. The final level is the common items that can be purchased "off-the-shelf." Scheduling the delivery of all procured products is critical because they will pace the "main line" of your implementation and integration activity.

Implementation consists of bringing all the elements together into a single system. Your people will be working together as a team and need to be evaluated both as individual performers and as team members. Using Personnel Management (22) techniques, you can keep up with individual performance in both these areas. This is important both to you for selecting people in the future and to the company for promotions and recognition.

It is necessary to use the concept of incremental testing due to the complexity of this and the levels that follow.

Final testing draws the entire system together and likely uses operators of the same level of abilities the customer will use. Sometimes the customer will require that the actual operating personnel be used to completely test the system. Also, all the elements of the system are used in final testing to ensure the system operates under the expected operating loads. If there are discrepancies, they must be captured in Discrepancy Reports (DRs) and dispositioned as Action Items (AIs) for closure. Treat AIs the same way as with intermediate systems. Again, run the final test a number of times before the customer arrives just to make sure the system will run properly during the real final test.

Closure Stage

The Closure Stage will have begun at final test just as with the intermediate project. It is usually a part of the Closure Stage to ensure that all the AIs are closed to the customer's satisfaction. Then it's time for handover, the Final Report, and the "Lessons Learned" paper.

Wrap up the project by having the customer sign off acceptance of the system. Once again, no matter what your internal procedures are, it is a good idea to have the customer sign off for the same reasons as before.

Finally, write a Final Report that summarizes the project. The Final Report usually goes to the customer and is filed internally. Additionally, write a "Lessons Learned" paper. Keeping personal copies of these papers will give you a library of things "to-do" and "not-to-do" in future.

You have phased your people in and out as with the intermediate project, so you should be down to a core team at this point.

A Program

In Chapter 4, I said that a program "is distinguished from a project by the existence of a legal contract between the company and the customer." So, in order to lead a program, you need to add all the subject areas of the Expert Skill Set to the knowledge you gained in the Basic and Advanced Skill Sets. Because your customer is now outside the company, we are no longer talking about a "slap on the wrist" if the project does not go exactly right. Here we are talking about a legal situation that, even if you win, will cost the company a significant sum of money. You need to know what you are doing contractually. One other very important task to be added to your responsibilities is that you now have profit and loss responsibility. I like to say that I have profit responsibility. I don't know what loss responsibility is because I've never had a losing program (ahem). OK, OK, OK (with apologies to Joe Pesci), let's take the pieces one by one.

As a consequence of these differences, you will need to add to your competencies Business Considerations (29), Legal Considerations (31), Customer Relations and Satisfaction (36), and Management Relations and Satisfaction (43), as well as a number of other related subject areas.

Figure 9-6 shows the characteristics of a program. Comparing this table to the tables presented for the other project and program types, you can see where the differences lie at just a glance. (Some of these may be contractual at the program level.)

Initiate Stage

In the earlier definition and discussion of the Initiate Stage, I said that a program is subdivided into three periods: the initiation phase, the pursuit phase, and the capture phase. In this case our discussion begins with the initiation phase. The initiation phase is the purview of the customer whether it is a project or a program. The customer creates a

Figure 9-6. Program characteristics.

Tasks:	Practically any task defined by an outside customer and awarded through a legal contract.
Customer:	The customer is outside the company. A legal contract exists between the customer and the company.
Value:	Usually greater than $5,000,000.
Duration:	Usually more than 1 year.
Risk Level:	Moderate to high.
Complexity:	Moderate to high.
Contract Type(s):	Can be any of the basic contract types for the overall contract. Some elements of the overall contract may be different types.
Number of People:	Usually more than 10.
Disciplines:	Multidisciplinary.
Schedule Tools:	Software applications, including enterprise software applications.
Accounting Base:	Dollars through profit.
Accounting Tools:	Time cards/sheets, invoices. Usually automated.
Organization Type:	Matrix or projectized.
PM Reports to:	Line manager or director and/or PMO.
Materials and Subcontracts:	Identified, procured, accounted for, and verified by program.
Quality:	Ad hoc or assigned depending on size and complexity.
Effectiveness:	Ad hoc or assigned depending on size and complexity.
Facilities and Equipment:	Identified by program, provided by company or, in some cases, the customer.
Team Training:	Involved. Several days. May include customer.
Applicable Skill Set:	Expert

need, documents the requirement, and, in the case of a program, puts the requirement up for bid. Marketing has identified and tracked the program, and the program has been qualified as a legitimate bid opportunity. As stated earlier, identifying opportunities is the purview of the marketing department. You may or may not be involved in identifying opportunities.

Once the requirement is issued however, the "troika" is established (see Glossary). As program manager, you assist the assigned marketer in tracking the new program. The marketer is primarily interested in the competition, the schedule for procurement release, the winning price, and the politics of the procurement. The technical manager is interested in the technology involved. If the enterprise has followed the Technology Management (32) plan and provided "on-ramps," you should be able to slip into this technology easily. If not, you may have a very difficult time or it might be time to no-bid. If the company has all the capabilities, including the technologies needed to perform this program, fine. If not, you may need to gain that knowledge through Teaming & Partnering (37) activity. It is likely that the marketing representative will initiate this activity, but you really need to manage it. This may create some friction, but if you were thorough in your Teaming & Partnering study, you will be able to handle it.

If all these factors are overcome, fine. If not, here is where the concepts of Value Management (27) come into play, and you must understand the positions of management and marketing and how they evaluate the position of this program. Why? Because it is possible that the program will be identified and qualified, and after the tracking process is started, new information is unveiled that makes the program a "no-bid." This is a very difficult time in programs, because just as soon as a program is identified to be tracked, it gains a personality. People identify with the personality, right or wrong, and don't want to let it go. You will hear arguments like you've never heard before about why you should continue with the bid process. Nevertheless, follow the precepts of value management and do what needs to be done.

When in a bid posture, you are primarily interested in the Statement of Work (SOW), the task to be accomplished, the people involved, the performance schedule, and any unusual considerations of any kind (programmatic, technical, or contractual). Notice that I used the term "primarily interested." This term is used to recognize the primary focus of the individual, not the overall interest. In fact, you, the marketer, and the technical person will each be interested in *all aspects of the entire program.*

How long you track the program depends on when the opportunity was identified and when the request will be issued. I have tracked some programs for many months and some for only a day or two. You should track the program long enough to present your capabilities to the customer and to fully understand all the wants and needs of the customer, plus any tidbits that may give you a competitive advantage.

During this time, you will be involved in making tactical alliances and teaming arrangements if necessary. In a classical case, let's assume you make a teaming arrangement with a small software company that has a unique product that meets a critical need to be included in the request. Your marketer has been clever enough to find this company and conduct teaming discussions. This small company will provide a "software kernel" around which you will wrap some entry and exit paths and imbed this software into the overall software package for the customer. You must monitor the process very carefully because there are implications of infringement into the intellectual product of both that company and the software your program develops. These issues may well test your Legal Considerations (31). You decide the lawyers need to be involved in drafting the teaming agreement. Both the marketer and the technical person agree. Clearly, you have a need for understanding Marketing and Sales (38) and Business Considerations (29).

Now your presentations to the customer involve not only you, but your new teammate as well. You have a new capability set to offer the customer. You continue these interfaces and data gathering until the requirement is issued. Once the requirement is issued, the procurement people get involved, and all contacts go to "arm's length." This means that the technical and program people will only talk to you through their procurement people. All these contacts are made "official" and are usually documented. This is the opportunity to understand and put into practice Customer Relations and Satisfaction (36).

Once the requirement has been issued, you are ready to start the proposal. Actually, the troika has been working with the Proposal Center for several months. If this is a very large program, you will be working with the entire proposal core team long before the request is issued.

The Proposal Center must be kept apprised of the requirement and its schedule—that is, the time when the requirement will be issued, when the proposal is due, what the proposal size is to be, and every other detail you can think of. The Finance Office must be kept apprised of the proposal needs as well. Your role will be challenged by how well you learned and applied the Financial Management (25) subject area. In fact, within twenty-four hours of when the request is received, you should be able to issue all the needs of the proposal: the schedule, section assignments, page allocations, the theme, and every other detail necessary to get the proposal published and back to the customer, including who delivers the proposal and when.

Your Proposals (39) training will have shown it is normal to treat a large proposal as if it were a program with kickoff, execution, and closure. For a proposal of this size, you need to have a proposal kickoff. You can assume that a person from the Proposal Center will be assigned as the overall proposal manager and that you will lead the Management Proposal and the Cost Proposal. A person assigned from the Finance Office will provide the support necessary for the financial "boilerplate" and will "crunch" the numbers as they come in. It is necessary for you to make sure the budgets are assigned and the numbers come in on schedule and on budget. They won't, so you'll need to stay on top of everyone that owes you cost data. The technical person (now the Chief Engineer) leads the Technical Proposal.

The proposal writing will be in process for some time and include the design of the product to meet the requirement, a review of the design, a costing of the design, a redesign to meet the cost envelope, and all the writing necessary. The drawings will pace the writing and production.

The most critical part of any proposal is the costing process. You need to know how to cost your part of the proposal and understand the cost bases of the other contributors as well. Estimating (33) techniques are required for your costs and for evaluating the cost inputs of others.

Finally, the writing is complete and the proposal will go through editing, rewriting, incorporation of the drawings, and ultimately printing. The marketing representative flies all night to deliver all seven boxes of the proposal to the customer just before the clock runs out.

The proposal phase is different and unique. Even though it is conducted the same as a program, there are numerous nuances that you must learn to conduct a proposal effort. Those details are outside the scope of this book but the seminars mentioned in Chapter 6 provide you with a base for participating on proposal teams until you gain the experience to conduct one of your own.

The customer reviews your proposal and usually has a number of questions to submit to you. This can, and frequently does, happen several times during the proposal evaluation. In some cases, you may be required to give an oral presentation and answer questions posed by the customer's evaluation team, in real time.

Finally, after iterations of questions and answers, the day comes. The customer representative calls the general manager of your company and tells him or her of the award. If the contract is large enough, the U.S. representative from your district calls the general manager with the news first. Time for another party—no pizza this time!

The time for negotiations has been set. You show up with the marketer, the chief engineer, a finance representative, and a contracts manager. After pleasantries, you get down to business. Then you discover that these guys are serious! How you handle all this depends on what you learned in the seminars you attended for Negotiations (40).

Finally, negotiations are complete, and you and your team return to the office. Exhausted but happy, you take the next day off to get your "faculties back in mind"[2] and rejoin the human race.

You were lucky. You were a part of the Capture Team, so you know what went on in the negotiations. Still, you need to document the findings of the negotiations just to make sure everyone knows what the program baseline is for Handoff (35).

Planning Stage

It's time to call the core team together and get the planning under way. The functional managers are "chomping at the bit" trying to get you to put the people on the program (meaning on your charge number and not their overhead), and you are trying to hold them off, but at the same time hold on to the people you want. This is going to take some diplomacy and maybe a few lunches. Get started. The objective is to get a Program Plan completed and approved, bring the team on board, provide team training, and have a kickoff for your team and for management as soon as possible.

First, establish your Mission Statement. Convene the core team and use the "Brainstorming Method" (Glossary) to create a Mission Statement with meaning to each and every one of you.

The Program Plan is the written instrument that summarizes and references the requirements of the customer and the requirements of the company to the team. It is the most important document you will create, and it must contain, in a company confidential attachment, the understandings you have with management, such as follow-on sales and profit. These issues will have been covered when researching Management Relations and Satisfaction (43).

Have roundtable meetings with the contracts manager, the finance representative, the chief engineer, and the subcontracts manager; and construct the framework for the Program Plan, then establish the Work Breakdown Structure (WBS) and name the subcontracts involved. Remember, if you have an alliance, that's the subcontract you want to nail down before anything else.

Then create the Organization Chart. One of the questions for the Organization Chart is where to put the alliance that was created. Are they part of the "voting" organization and placed within the organizational structure? Or are they treated as a subcontractor and placed on an extension below the primary organization chart? These questions have political overtones and will have a bearing on how the overall organization operates.

At this point, you can release the core team to return to their functions and "farm out" various sections of the Program Plan, with specific instructions, just like what was done with the proposal. Each must perform their functions and get back together quickly. Remember, this is the plan and not the actual design or the actual subcontracts. You need to maintain control to ensure the Program Plan process does not exceed its bounds and slip into design or otherwise go off track. Once you have the Program Plan established, together with the WBS and the Organization Chart, you are ready to start bringing the people on board.

For lower-level projects, we used Earned Value Management (18) techniques to understand project performance. We now need to add more refined techniques through the use of Metrics (26).

Larger programs imply more people and a concentrated workplace. Here is where you need to make considerations of Health, Safety, Security & Environmental (28) factors of the workplace.

For training, bring everyone together. For a group this size, I recommend you have a warm-up to get everyone comfortable with everyone else. You can do this and make some progress at the same time by using the Myers-Briggs Type Indicator (MBTI) program as described in Chapter 8.

To get ready for a kickoff for this program, each group must put together all the work packages for which it is responsible. The Work Package has task, schedule, and budget, and should be a line item on the overall program schedule. This is the level that should be presented at the team kickoff. When presenting to management and to the customer, present at the level required by the contract.

It is a good idea for a program such as this to formalize the kickoff meeting. This means giving a stand-up presentation with visual aids. The team presentation is a good preliminary run for the management or customer presentation. By the way, if the management or customer reviews are not required, you should still conduct a full-blown kickoff meeting for a program of this size. In this case, you and the core team are the reviewing authority.

Execution Stage

The Execution Stage for these programs includes a number of progressive periods, and some of these periods are subdivided into even finer increments. In addition, there is some overlap between the periods as well as with the phases. To complicate matters even further, you may be going through a design period on one subsystem and the development period with another subsystem. But that's what keeps program management interesting.

The Design Period will likely be subdivided into subsystem designs and a system design. The system will likely have several design reviews such as a Conceptual Design Review (Concept). The system and each subsystem will have incremental design reviews, such as a Preliminary Design Review (PDR), a Critical Design Review (CDR), and a Final Design Review (FDR). Each is conducted in strict accordance with established procedures. The chief engineer manages the reviews but you must attend them all and be aware of all the details. Each period must have Design & Development (30) considerations, and activities must meet the "gates" established before proceeding any further. As each design review is completed with the customer in attendance, you should have the customer sign an acceptance sheet to attach to the design package for your records. I have found it is essential to either take notes myself or have a very trusted team member take them. These include not only formal action items, but anything helpful in avoiding problems or satisfying a customer. Each subsystem design review must precede the equal system design review. In other words, all the subsystem PDRs must be completed before the system PDR is conducted, and so on. This assumes the subsystems are a part of the overall system. If a subsystem is "outboard" of the main system, its design reviews can be conducted independently. If that is confusing, consider that related systems and subsystems are sometimes collected together under the aegis of one program. That's what I am talking about here.

With a great number of people with diverse personalities and with different technical and administrative objectives (read: agendas), you are certain to encounter conflict somewhere along the path. This may happen occasionally or frequently. How often it happens may well be a reflection on how well you prepared the individuals as a team. Nevertheless, conflicts will arise, and you must control them with the Conflict Management (41) techniques you learned to be a part of the program.

In one form or another, programs of this size use Prototyping (34) as a method of execution to get the product to market as soon as possible. Prototyping can be a great advantage or can blow up in your face. As program manager, you must stay on top of any prototyping activities that are going on and avoid disasters through forward thinking.

The Procurement Period will begin almost immediately after the contract has been awarded. These procurements are a part of the design in the proposal, and now it is time to get the "Best and Final" proposals from the competitors. It is also time to finalize any Teaming Agreements you may have entered into during the Initial Stage. It is amazing how your leverage increases with subs after you've won a contract.

Engineering writes the specifications, the Program Office (that's you) writes the Statements of Work, and the Subcontract Manager writes the Terms and Conditions (Ts & Cs). Subcontracts then go through the accepted practices of advertising, proposal evaluation, and award for the subcontracts outstanding.

As the design develops, engineering develops a materials list. This is a "living list" and will be updated frequently. The Materials Manager combines all the lists at the appropriate time and order for volume.

Here is where the (in)famous 80/20 rule comes into play. You know, the one that says: "You spend the first 80 percent of the money on the first 80 percent of the program and the next 80 percent of the money on the last 20 percent of the program." This is the point where it starts to rear its head. Your job as program manager here will be a constant state of "work arounds." Whatever plan you had yesterday needs to be modified today because something "doesn't fit right." This period will try your problem-solving skills, and once again, you and your chief engineer will be living in each other's pockets.

You are a clever and hardworking person (ahem!) and you will manage to get through even this. Until you are challenged, you can't really understand what success is.

Testing is progressive, and its importance rises in visibility at this point. The customer is apprised of system test schedules, and you provide the test procedures sometime before the test is to begin. The usual process is to send out the test procedures about sixty to ninety days before system test and allow thirty days for comments. When comments begin to come back, you will find that some of the people who have been sleeping for the last year are suddenly awake. They are asking questions and making comments that are a year old. This is the point where your "diplomatic self" needs to come to the front. Handle these comments as best you can. Refer back to the documentation you have kept throughout the program to show your position. Sometimes even this won't work, and people become emotional. You need to handle these emotional outbursts on a logical level. To say: "It's not that we won't make the changes, it's just that the change will cost X dollars and Y months in the schedule" is the way you handle these issues. Changes at this point are very expensive. I have seen programs go berserk at this stage, and getting to agreement will test every ounce of diplomatic, psychological, and technical skills you can muster. Don't be afraid to ask for help.

You have been leading your program team confidently, and when you enter final system test, you are ready. The team is assembled, the hardware and software have been successfully interfaced a number of times. The procedures have been run, red-lined, rewritten, and rerun. The customer is here, and you are ready for the final system test.

Even when everything runs well, there may be some minor glitches that weren't caught earlier, or the customer suddenly decides he wants to see another aspect of the operation. These call for Action Items (AIs). Document the anomalies or changes and work them off until everyone is satisfied. All this must be kept in scope however. If not, the change may present an opportunity for a contract expansion, Engineering Change Proposal (ECP) (Glossary), or follow-on work.

Closure Stage

You are finally here. Now, it's a mixture of emotions. On the one hand, you're glad it's behind you, and it has been a successful program. On the other hand, the team members are going their separate ways. You have developed a close relationship with each of them, and they with you, over the life of the program. Now you have a retinue of folks who will be glad to work with you on any program in the future. That's a great feeling!

The Closure Stage began during the testing phase to ensure that all the AIs got documented and worked off. And they were. Now is the time for handover to the customer.

There are some formal legal documents to sign for the system and for the security equipment and software. The chief engineer, the contracts manager, and you sign these documents. The system then belongs to the customer.

You have taken care of your people by "shedding" them at appropriate times throughout the program. Early in the program, you released the design engineers who completed their tasks. The Configuration Management (CM), quality, and Reliability, Maintainability and Availability (RMA) people were just brought on for specific tasks, and you won't need to worry about them. At this point, you should have just enough people to get through the system test and perform the wrap-up. You should be back to the core team again, just as when you started. It's a good time to have each member of the core team write up their "Lessons Learned" paper and give them to you. Combine and refine the inputs and create a final "Lessons Learned" paper that you turn over to your boss, and of course, keep a copy for yourself. Not only for records purposes but for reminders of changes you can make to processes and procedures when in a position to do so.

Now is a good time to write thank-you letters to all those who participated in the program and letters of commendation for those who did outstanding jobs. If you didn't do this when it happened, you need to do it now. Little things like photos of the final product in action are greatly appreciated by the people and don't cost a lot. One of the things that you can use is a "Certificate of Accomplishment" or the like. With today's computers and ten cents' worth of certificate material from the local stationery store, you can create a handsome certificate with appropriate lettering to acknowledge a person's actions. I assure you, people hang these on the wall. This investment will return tenfold on the next program. You can bet these people will be willing to work with you on the next job that comes down the pike.

You met all your cost and profit objectives. The best part is that you have given your customer a good product, you have given the company a good profit, and have created a good reputation for yourself, so you will go up a few notches when the next, larger program comes along. That's a good feeling, and that's what it's all about!

A Virtual Project or Program

The only thing in life that is constant is change! I don't know who said it first but it was probably on day two after Creation. Just when we think we can play the game, they go and change the rules. As I said in Chapter 3, projects and programs are becoming more and more virtual. This project type is presented for several reasons: First, many projects are now using this technique in some form. Second, the world of pure software is moving more and more in this direction, and you may well be confronted with a project of this sort. Third, you may want to add this kind of thinking to some of your projects or programs at this point in your career. Is this a better way to handle your subcontractors? Can you use some of these techniques on your spread-out home campus to increase efficiency? To decrease costs? Virtual Projects are complex and evolving. They will be the subject of many more books in the future. The following however is intended only to show the differences between a virtual project and a traditional project.

Any virtual project needs three primary project tools to accomplish the task. The first is a communications tool. The second is a project management tool. The third is a construct tool.

Communications Tool. It is generally agreed in the virtual world that e-mail is the quick reaction tool of choice for this task. However, a virtual project of any size needs a "home" or "war room" where the current status of the elements of the project can be seen, and a "water cooler" section for topics for discussion. Of course, each project will have its own format and content dictated by the nature of the project at hand. Whatever the format, this tool is the Web site. It can be on an intranet, such as a company LAN, or an extranet, such as a company WAN, or the Internet.

Project Management Tool. There are several project management tools available on the market that lend themselves to virtual projects such as Microsoft Project, Primavera, and Project Scheduler. A generalized summary of the data in the tool can be presented on the project Web site. The mechanics of the project management tool will allow the project manager to keep up with the entire project in a form normally used. Even though you can "parse" out the elements of the management tool, there is one thing that absolutely must be common in a virtual project—that is, every function must "sign up" to the task they are to perform. This is a normal function during the teaming session, and the results should be posted on the project Web site.

Technical Tool. Here's where it gets tough. Is there a common tool that all the technical people on the virtual project are familiar with and can operate within? It depends. If the virtual project or program is within one company, a multinational, for instance, it is possible that a common set of tools will be used, because companies tend to standardize on tools for economic and legal (licensing) reasons. But, for a project that is put together by dissemination and bidding, there is usually no way everyone will be using the same tools. Not only will the tools be different, the languages will be different as well. The emergence and refinement of the Java language is helping to commonize these tools, but we are still a long way from a standard language or tools. Furthermore, hardware programs will probably use some basic tool such as CAD or AutoCad, while software programs will likely use tools specific to the task. The only way to ensure that the tools are common is to specify the tools to be used. This will likely be expensive to start but will most certainly save money and time in the long run.

Figure 9-7 shows the characteristics of a virtual program. Comparing this table with the tables presented for the other project and program types, you can see where the differences lie at just a glance.

Planning Stage

The Planning Stage of this project is critical, even more so than on a normal project or program. The communication and control of the entire project must be thought through before the project is launched and then presented in the Project Plan. The Project Plan must be written or controlled such that it can be available to everyone and yet not expose trade secrets to the competition. One of the best ways I know of to do this is to establish a secure Web site. The level of security should be consistent with the value of the data contained on the Web site. No more, no less.

First, look around. Are there other projects that have been conducted in your company using this method? If so, search out the project plan used for that project and modify it to your needs. You should probably allow for more time than usual to develop your plan and to leave time for more iterations. The most common characteristic of virtual projects is that they are all a little different.

Figure 9-7. Virtual project or program characteristics.

Tasks:	Any task that requires geographically separate work locations.
Customer:	For a project: Follows the characteristics of a large project. For a program: Follows the characteristics of a program.
Value:	Variable.*
Duration:	Usually more than 1 year.
Risk Level:	Moderate to very high.
Complexity:	Moderate to very high.
Contract Type(s):	If a project, no contract. If a program, any type of contract with or without incentive or award provisions.
Number of People:	Usually more than 10.
Disciplines:	Multidisciplinary.
Schedule Tools:	Software applications compatible with Internet transmission.
Accounting Base:	If a project: hours. If a program: dollars.
Accounting Tools:	May be disparate in that more than one company is involved. Usually complex and requires time for collection and reconciling.
Organization Type:	Matrix or projectized.
PM Reports to:	Line manager or director and/or PMO.
Materials and Subcontracts:	Identified, procured, accounted for, and verified by program.
Quality:	Ad hoc or assigned depending on size and complexity.
Effectiveness:	Ad hoc or assigned depending on size and complexity.
Facilities and Equipment:	Identified by program, provided by affected company, or in some cases, the customer.
Team Training:	Involved. Several days. May include customer.
Applicable Skill Set:	Expert

*Becoming more and more common even for smaller tasks.

The project plan for a virtual project must be comprehensive, thorough, and thought through (read that sentence slowly). Everyone on the team must know not only what he or she is doing but what every other team member is doing as well. As I said earlier, each function must sign up to their task, and that information must be available to the entire team on the project Web site.

In this case, the team is dictated to you. The team is established and the people and locations apprised of the need for support. Your job begins by convening the group, making a team of them, and getting the job done. This is the time and place for the team to meet and interchange electronically in the same way they would if they were meeting face-to-face.

Training a virtual team is the same and different. It is the same in that each person describes the inputs they need to do their job and the expectations they have of others regarding inputs. It is different in that it is not done in "real-time." The nature of e-mail is that it is asynchronous—that is, response is not immediate to the question. An exception to this is made by the use of "chat rooms" to get everyone online at the same time. In chat rooms, statements or questions and responses are in near real-time.

Training begins by "broadcasting" all the necessary materials, such as vision, Mission Statement, requirements, and documents to all the team members and asking for comments. Resolve the comments and go on to the team interfacing portion, where each team member states their needs and expectations. A chat room environment is a good tool to use if brainstorming is needed. You can set up a chat room at a time most convenient to all the team members. Sometimes this is very difficult, especially if unions are involved (when it is noon here, it is midnight somewhere else, and overtime may be required), and you must also be sensitive to the observance of different cultural and religious days. This point will test your application of Social Sensitivity (42). At any rate, set up your chat room and get on and off as quickly as possible. Another method to use is a conference call. And finally, a video link can be used. Internet video linking currently gives marginal results, but gets better all the time. Advances in compression technology are refining this mode, so it is a good idea to keep up with the latest available.

Once all the training needs and issues have been met, they should be captured and placed in a reference section of the project Web site for future reference.

You will likely need to provide absolute assurance to your management that your virtual project is ready to kick off. But before proceeding, be sure that management concurs with all the objectives, goals, strategies, schedules, and so on. Conduct your kickoff electronically exactly as you would in a face-to-face situation. Once launched, virtual projects are much more difficult and confusing to change than traditional projects. When the project is launched, announce to the other team members that they may now charge to the Execution Stage of this project.

Execution Stage

The Execution Stage of this project is accomplished in a very traditional manner—that is, design is completed before coding begins. The product is tested, and the process iterated as necessary. Granted, your project may not be conducted in this manner but the purpose in this section is to show differences between traditional and virtual project—not to make life harder!

Techniques such as rapid prototyping, build-a-little/test-a-little, peer review, and code exchange should be emphasized to enhance the probability of success.

The major difficulty you will face in the Execution Stage is, once again, communication. In this case (and this is quite common) the coding is done in a "tank" full of people. Your communication is through the local project supervisor only—he or she may be the only one who speaks your language. Using some of the techniques recommended above will help overcome this situation.

Sometimes the gain in labor costs is offset by the cost of rework, so be very careful and most explicit in your directions.

Closure Stage

The important part of the Closure Stage is delivering the product and all of its documentation. Further, a final report and especially a "Lessons Learned" paper are in order. This is particularly true if this is the first such project conducted in your company, or the first one you have led, or there was something else unusual about it.

One of the neat things about a project such as this is that the people just fade away. You don't need to worry about sending them back to their home units because they never left in the first place. However, a few words of caution: Make certain that the product has been accepted by the customer before closing the project. It can be extremely expensive to try to restart a project such as this.

An International Program

An international program is a different kind of beast. An international program should be led only by a program manager specifically trained or with specific experience in international programs. Additionally, the program manager should be aware of the specific rules required by his or her own country when dealing with the customer's country and the specific rules that apply to this program in the customer's country. It is likely that they will not be the same.

An international program follows the same precepts as a regular program insofar as the definitions are concerned. But the devil, as they say, is in the details.

Figure 9-8 shows the characteristics of an international program. Comparing this table to the tables presented for the other project and program types, you can see where the differences lie at just a glance.

Initiate Stage

The Initiate Stage follows the same guidelines as for the normal program except that the Initiate Stage is usually longer, a lot longer, and is usually handled primarily by an in-country marketing representative or agent. The expense of international travel is a real factor in pursuing these kinds of programs.

As stated earlier, identifying opportunities is usually the purview of the marketing department, in this case, the in-country marketing representative or agent. The in-country marketing representative usually lives with the customer and understands the cultural nuances as well as the special considerations of the customer's procurement processes. We will likely not be involved in identifying opportunities.

Once a program has been identified and selected is where the "troika" is established, just as in a regular program. The primary difference is that the marketer will be "in country" or living with the customer, and the program manager and technical manager will stay CONUS (i.e., the continental United States). As program manager, you will assist the assigned marketer in tracking the new program. The marketer is primarily interested in the competition, the schedule for procurement release, the winning price, and the politics of the procurement. You, on the other hand, are primarily interested in the Statement

Figure 9-8. International program characteristics.

Tasks:	Any task that requires delivery of the product to an overseas location.
Customer:	For a project: Follows the characteristics of a large project. For a program: Follows the characteristics of a program.
Value:	Usually greater than $5,000,000.
Duration:	Usually more than 1 year.
Risk Level:	Moderate to very high.
Complexity:	Moderate to very high.
Contract Type(s):	Any of the basic contract types plus international letters of credit with draw-down provisions.
Number of People:	Usually more than 10.
Disciplines:	Multidisciplinary.
Schedule Tools:	Software applications compatible with Internet transmission.
Accounting Base:	Time cards/sheets, invoices, international clearinghouse invoices. Payment may be in customer currency, provider currency, third-party currency, or in bartered goods as agreed to in the contract.
Accounting Tools:	Direct payment, payment through in-country agents, or international bank accountability, or a combination of means.
Organization Type:	Matrix or projectized.
PM Reports to:	Line manager or director and/or PMO.

(continues)

Figure 9-8. (Continued).

Materials and Subcontracts:	Identified, procured, accounted for, and verified by program. May be purchased internationally and drop shipped or trans shipped.
Quality:	Ad hoc or assigned.
Effectiveness:	Ad hoc or assigned.
Facilities and Equipment:	Usually defined by the program and provided by the company.
Team Training:	Same as program but usually does not include the customer.
Applicable Skill Set:	Specialty

of Work (SOW), the task to be accomplished, the people involved, the performance schedule, and any unusual considerations of any kind (programmatic, technical, or contractual). The technical person is primarily interested in the specification for the product, just the same as in a normal program.

How long you track the program depends on when the opportunity was identified and when the request is issued, but you can expect that the tracking period will be over a long time. How the requirement is conceived and how it develops are two of the unusual things that happen in international programs. If alliances develop, your understanding of Teaming and Partnering (37), Business Considerations (29), and Marketing and Sales (38), as well as a number of other subject areas, will be tested.

Now your presentations to the customer take on a new flair. Your teammate will be involved in your presentations even if by name only. You must be extremely careful with this type of arrangement. The alliance partner will know that he has been demanded by the customer and will likely act accordingly. In other words, you may well lose your prime/sub leverage.

After the requirement is issued, you are ready to start the proposal. This will be a moderately sized proposal but follows essentially the same path as the other program proposals. Sometimes, the price is dictated by the customer, and you need to figure out how to meet the needs of the requirement as well as making the price work. This is called a "design to cost" program. It is necessary for you to make sure the budgets are assigned and the numbers come in on schedule and on budget. Of course they won't, so you need to stay on top of everyone that owes you cost data.

During this time, the in-country marketing representative will have been working the payment schemes. It is not unusual in international procurements to be paid in the currency of the country with which you are doing business. Now, you may be thinking, "So what? I can exchange dinars or ryals for dollars almost anywhere." Yes, that's true, but what if you are being paid in lumber? Specialists will need to figure out the bartering arrangements to get to dollars; it may take several "trades." When you finally do get to some recognized currency, you will likely need insurance to "hedge" the exchange rate. In some technology areas, the U.S. Defense Department or State Department will have regulations on what technology can be exported or what can not. It's worth knowing if this is a possible barrier before investing too much. See what I mean about the "nuances" of international programs?

You will likely send the proposal through a recognized international, rapid-delivery service to the in-country marketing representative. The rep will hand-carry the proposal to the customer with some amount of ceremony and a cup of tea. The in-country representative uses this opportunity for another interface meeting. The customer may evaluate the proposal or it may be a fait accompli. After some period of time, you will get a "turn on" for the task.

The negotiation will likely be handled by the in-country marketing representative with questions being sent to you via email or fax. Have the team answer the questions and return the answers using the same medium. Often you will need to convene the support team at unusual times because of the time differences between the host country and the providing country.

Hopefully, you were a part of the Capture Team and on top of the procurement every moment so you know what went on in the negotiations. You need to work with the in-country representative to document the findings of the negotiations just to make sure everyone knows what the program baseline is.

Planning Stage

The Planning Stage follows the same general path as a standard program. The objective is to get a Program Plan completed and approved, bring the team on board, provide team training, and have a kickoff for your team and for management as soon as possible.

This Program Plan has a few hard points that need mentioning. The hard points usually are: customer meetings, transportation, drop shipment, port handling, taxes, fees, cartage and drayage, and local labor. Leave plenty of time in your schedule for these activities because very few other countries in the world have the same sense of schedule urgency as the English-speaking countries, with the possible exception of some European countries. Dock waits and customs can be program killers, and you will probably need an in-country agent (frequently different from the marketing representative) to make these things happen.

Have roundtable meetings with the contracts manager, the finance representative, the chief engineer, the subcontracts manager, and the in-country representative, and construct the framework for the Program Plan. Then, establish the Work Breakdown Structure (WBS) and name the subcontracts to be involved. Remember, you have an alliance, and that's the subcontract you want to nail down before anything else. Then you want to create the Organization Chart. One of the questions for the Organization Chart is where to put the alliance that was created. All this will test your knowledge of Structures (14), Organization (19), Teaming & Partnering (37), and Negotiation (40), at least.

Once you have the Program Plan established, together with the WBS and the Organization Chart, you are ready to start bringing the people on board.

In the case of this task, your major team members will be dedicated but your program will not be projectized.

For training, follow the details of a program.

The kickoff for an international program is handled in the same way as a standard program. If possible, have a customer representative and the in-country representative attend the kickoff and let them understand where the hard spots and milestones are in the program.

Execution Stage

As the "honeymoon period" fades, this program will likely have more problems than in a standard program, mainly because of the distance problem. A technique I have used to minimize the distance problem is to provide photographs with the monthly reports to the customer. This gives the customer something "nearly tangible" to hold on to and not feel left out of the process. Nevertheless, as you near the end of the program, the customer realizes he will be accepting this "thing" and will be responsible for it from here on. Questions and comments that should have been asked and answered in the design reviews and status meetings will suddenly take on a new level of intensity. Your position must be to document everything throughout the various periods so that, when this happens, you are ready.

Your design period follows the same sequences and requirements as the standard program.

The procurement period begins almost immediately after. It is also time to finalize the Teaming Agreement. Pay special attention to the international procurements and to drop shipping and trans shipping.

There may be special considerations for the procurements where the products will be produced in one country, shipped here, and integrated into the product that will be delivered to your customer in yet a third country. You and your procurement specialists will have a jolly good time working out all the import/export and use agreements, but this is fun stuff!

The implementation period comes next. When dealing with materials and software that are procured internationally, things that work well alone don't always interface properly, even when all the design interfaces and Interface Control Documents (ICDs) are followed. Many things happen, and some require significant rework and retest. All that of course takes time.

Your job as program manager here will be a constant state of "work arounds." Whatever plan you had yesterday needs to be modified today because something "doesn't fit right." This period will try your problem-solving skills, and once again, you and your chief engineer will be living in each other's pockets.

The testing period really goes on throughout the entire program. Component tests, subassembly tests, and subsystem tests have been going on since early in the program. You and the chief engineer will constantly stay in contact with the test engineer to ensure that there is a lineage of tests and they are all accounted for.

Testing is progressive and incremental, and its importance rises in visibility at this point. As in standard programs, you apprise the customer of system test schedules and provide the test procedures some time before the test is to begin.

On international programs, a funny thing frequently happens about this time. The customer representative that was sent to witness the tests has some personal likes of his own. He wants you to change from what was specified to what he likes. This is a time when your "diplomatic self" needs to come to the front. Handle these comments as best you can. Refer to the documentation you have kept throughout the program to show your position. Sometimes even this will not work, and people get emotional. On international programs you may need to make critical decisions at this point. Because there will be political overtones, don't be afraid to ask for help.

As in previous programs, you have been leading your program carefully, and when you enter final system test, you are ready. The procedures have been run, red-lined, rewritten, and rerun. The customer is here, and you are ready for the final system test.

Document the anomalies or changes and work them off until everyone is satisfied. As before, all this must be in scope.

Now is the time to ship to the customer. It is necessary to get the units to a point of embarkation, on the ships or airplanes and transported to the customer's country. Now is when the in-country agent becomes worth his weight in gold. You need to move the units from the port to the delivery point. Duties need to be paid, and, in some cases, local contracts and "accommodations" are required. You have been isolated from all this by your agent. The agent does this every day, and it is within his operating methods to do so.

You may send members of your staff to the customer's country to retest the units and ensure that you are delivering a compliant product to the customer. All is well. The customer is satisfied, and the in-country representative is overjoyed. This gives him something to point to with pride whenever visiting the customer and will likely lead to more business. After all, that's why we do what we do!

Closure Stage

There are some formal, legal documents to sign for the system, usually more than the norm. You, the chief engineer, and the contracts manager (and maybe the security person) will sign these documents, and the system belongs to the customer. Some of the documents must be sent to the Department of State or other high-level agencies to close out the program.

As usual, take care of your people by "shedding" them at appropriate times throughout the program. It's a good time to have each team member write up their "Lessons Learned" and give them to you.

Combine and refine the inputs, create a final "Lessons Learned" paper, turn it over to your boss, and save a copy for your own files for later use.

Now is a good time to write thank-you letters to all those who participated in the program and letters of commendation for those who did outstanding jobs. If you didn't do this when it happened, you need to do it now. You can bet these people will be willing to work with you on the next job that comes down the pike.

You met all your cost and profit objectives even though it was touch and go for most of the program. You made some real-time judgments that reduced cost without impacting the product. Best of all you have given your customer a good product, you have given the company a good profit, and you have created a good reputation for yourself, so you will go up a few notches when the next, larger program comes along. That's a good feeling and it will stay with you for a long time.

A Large-Scale Project or Program

This is the one you've been waiting and training for. This is as good as it gets. Based on your performance on the last program you led, you're now ready for the big one. Now, instead of having a bunch of little problems plaguing you, you have a bunch of big problems plaguing you! We are talking about a large-scale program here—large-scale projects are few and far between and are almost exclusively the purview of the federal or at least the state government directly as a project or indirectly through contract as a program.

Even though your job is primarily a task of managing managers, you still have to sweat the small stuff. One small integrated circuit problem by a sub-sub-contractor can stop your entire program—dead in the water.

Figure 9-9 shows the characteristics of a large-scale program. Comparing this table to the tables presented for the other project and program types, you can see where the differences lie at just a glance.

Initiate Stage

The big difference between a program and a large-scale program in the Initiate Stage is that the Capture Team for a large-scale program is not only larger but also contains more disciplines. Frequently in a large-scale program, the proposal is nearly finished before the requirement is issued. The requirement may be in the form of a Request For Pro-

Figure 9-9. Large-scale project or program characteristics.

Tasks:	A large-scale system.
Customer:	For a project—Follows the characteristics of a large project. For a program: Follows the characteristics of a program.
Value:	Usually greater than $25,000,000.
Duration:	Usually more than 2 years.
Risk Level:	Moderate to very high.
Complexity:	Moderate to very high.
Contract Type(s):	Any combination of contract types. Frequently a mix.
Number of People:	Usually more than 50.
Disciplines:	Multidisciplinary.
Schedule Tools:	Enterprise-level automated software.
Accounting Base:	Dollars.
Accounting Tools:	Time cards/sheets, invoices. Will use a common, company-wide tool and is usually automated.
Organization Type:	Projectized but may draw upon specialists from other organizations.
PM Reports to:	Division General Manager or Group President, etc.
Materials and Subcontracts:	Identified, procured, accounted for, and verified by program.
Quality:	Assigned.
Effectiveness:	Assigned.

Facilities and Equipment:	Identified by the program. May be provided by parent company, purchased to support the program, provided by the customer, or a mixture of all three.
Team Training:	Involved. Subteams will be trained in groups, management personnel as a separate group. Training is constant and at a high level.
Applicable Skill Set:	Principal

posal (RFP) or a Request For Quotation (RFQ), or, in international terms, a Tender. The technical proposal consists of volumes and volumes, the management proposal is large, and the cost proposal goes on forever with costs being presented in at least four different ways. Frequently, everything has classified appendixes.

Every company has its own methods and techniques for identifying opportunities. Usually, large programs, such as this one, are initially identified by a corporate marketing office colocated with a primary customer somewhere. After identification and qualification, the program is usually assigned to a specific division of the corporation.

Tracking opportunities are usually left to the assigned division with the division marketer in the lead and the corporate marketer in attendance whenever you meet with the customer. If you think the feudal system was possessive, just wait until you see how the collocated marketer operates. Sometimes they seem to be more customer than company. They are unusually possessive of their customer because they have other divisions vying for other opportunities and because their raises and bonuses are dependent on how well you interface with "their" customer. Who wouldn't be possessive under these circumstances?

Most customers operate at "arm's length." That means they share with you enough information to get the best they can out of you. You must understand that everything the customer tells you, he has probably told someone else. The federal government, through the FARs, requires this posture. You or a member of your capture team may be able to pick up some critical piece of information that gives you an edge, but the customer won't usually give you an edge willingly. Tracking is a sophisticated process, and unless you have in-depth knowledge of the process, it is best to leave the strategizing up to the marketer in charge of the program.

Tracking begins once the program has been qualified and continues on through the proposal until award. Truthfully, tracking continues on even after award, because it allows the marketers a different level of access and perhaps more opportunity to find other programs. That's what they get paid for.

Bidding an opportunity begins with a top-down strategy. What is the strategy to be: best technical or lowest cost (usually it is both), and most frequently, the strategy must be "best value to the customer." Can we create a winning strategy using our technical and programmatic expertise that other competitors do not have? Do we have leverage through a unique alliance or team? This is serious business. This is the point where a program is won or lost because the proposal will follow the strategy set here. If you've got it all together, this is the point to create the Executive Summary for your proposal. A summary before the document is written? The short answer is yes! The tactics of the proposal must follow some direction. That direction is set in the Executive Summary. If you can't define the winning strategy at this point, try again or no-bid. Proposals are expensive endeavors. Guard the secrecy of this Executive Summary with your life—it's that important. Limit the availability to just a few people. Chances are, you learned all this and then some when attending seminars that supported Proposals (39).

After the proposal is written, you will update the Executive Summary, and this time, it will be a true summary. However, the strategy you devised at the outset will have been worked into a "Features and Benefits" section, and the rest will be a real summary of the proposal.

"It was the best of times, it was the worst of times . . ."[3] Not only does this opening establish the literary nature of a proposal, it establishes the trying nature of proposals as well. Proposals open with excitement, sink to despair, and end in trauma. During my first proposal, a friend of mine, Harry Gull, said: "You never get through writing a proposal—you just run out of time and print." How right he was. During my career, I have written hundreds of proposals, and it seems, no matter how well organized the proposal, there's always just one more change to be made. You know that the proposal is the lifeblood of the organization, and if you make just one more change it will be the difference between winning and not winning. In the proposal cycle, you never lose, you just don't win.

The most difficult part of any proposal is costing. You must start your costing early and from the top down, or you will end up with such a mess you'll never recover. Allocate cost to the various elements and then start arguing. Believe me, you will argue. Keep some dollars in your pocket for reserve and allocate them only at the last minute when you can't make everything add up. When you get to this point, I suggest you read paragraph 8.2.4 in my book *Blueprint for Project Recovery*. It offers some insight into how to maintain a risk reserve. Start costing as early as you can and then on a rigorous schedule. You'll still probably end up short on time. With the use of computers nowadays, costing should be a lot easier, but it really isn't. The emphasis now is in refinement rather than development.

After the proposal has been submitted, the customer's team will evaluate it. There will be questions and answers and maybe even oral presentations. Your job is to keep up the momentum, keep the people happy and creative and ready for the next round of questions. They will likely return to their operating positions at this point, so your job of keeping them happy will be a tough one.

The customer will go into what seems like hibernation (actually they are working just as hard as you did on the proposal) and for what seems like a long time. Other business will occupy the team members in the meantime. Your job is to pull the required members of the proposal team back together, brief them on the current situation, and respond to current needs. Most likely, you will need the team members more than once to answer questions that arise during proposal evaluation and then during negotiation. These questions must be answered immediately.

As stated earlier in this chapter, there is a balancing act between the marketing representative and the program person. Cost is the issue, particularly if you are still competing. You've got to win, but you've got to run the program too. Good luck! That's the subject for several more books.

It is your job to ensure that good minutes are kept of the negotiation so that a "data trail" exists between the proposal and the final contract. When negotiations are over, everything should be documented and made ready for handover.

If there has been execution team representation during the pursuit and the proposal, handover should be relatively easy. If there is a gap, it will be difficult. The execution team must know exactly what it's up against when running the program. You may be asking yourself right now, "Why doesn't the execution team just read the contract?" Although this sounds easy, it may not be. There are likely nuances that were uncovered during negotiation that contribute to the changes made from the proposal to the contract. The execution team needs to know these nuances. Unfortunately, there may have been off-line agreements made and not documented. This happens all the time. Remember when I talked about how the colocated marketer operates? The execution team needs to know about these agreements.

If handover has been properly conducted, the capture team should be able to fade away, and the execution team begins its "ramp-up" by starting the Planning Stage.

Planning Stage

The core team will already be identified, as will the critical program managers. The directors will be in place. The remainder of the staff, however, must be phased in as required. Training will be complex and ongoing for this program. The kickoff meeting will be formal and last for several days.

The Program Plan for this program will be significant. The Program Plan is developed first as an executive-level plan, and then a separate plan for each Subsystem Program Office (SPO) is developed. The core team for each subsystem develops an SPO program plan for their respective subsystems. The volumes of the Program Plan however are ordered by the way the organization is structured—that is, each program manager has their own program plan, and each of these plans will "roll up" into the overall program plan. Sort of a giant WBS.

This is an important point. The schedules presented in each of the program plans must contribute to the overall plan. An enterprise-oriented scheduling application must be used to accommodate all the various parts of the overall Master Program Plan. Even though individual inputs are allowed by the application, all inputs in this case are made by a central scheduling office to ensure consistency.

Now it is time to assemble the team. The overall team is defined in the proposal for the purposes of costing. It is likely that only the critical positions are named and resumes provided for them. The others appear simply as proposed levels and numbers. The levels indicate the cost of each position. It is not unusual to change the team composition after award as you gain insight into what must be done and reality is upon you. It has been months and months since the proposal was submitted, and some of the people have left the company and some have been consumed by other duties. If this is a cost plus program, you may need to report the new organization to the customer. The core team and the management team should remain constant, however, unless something dramatic happens during negotiation.

The complexity of this task will keep the personnel director and staff working overtime. Personnel will be taken from other divisions and from the outside. It is not unusual for a program of this magnitude to "draft" people from other divisions. Of course, this creates problems in the other divisions because the new program drafts the best from the divisions. Sometimes this process involves you negotiating releases with other vice presidents or general managers in the company. Sometimes this will stall and must be elevated to the next level for resolution. You must be prepared with the Scarlet O'Hara speech. You know: "Rhett, if I don't get the dress, it's curtains!" Only this time it's "If we don't get so-and-so, the program will fail, and you (the authority) won't make your numbers!"

Training in this program is different from training for smaller programs and projects. Not just because it is larger, but because programs of this size develop the leadership for subsequent programs.

For training, first bring the core team and the staff together. This includes the directors and all the SPO program managers. Again, I recommend you use the Myers-Briggs Type Indicator (MBTI) program (see Chapter 8) as an opener. Follow this up with the training necessary for the program. This training includes the Mission Statement, the customer, the organization, and the requirements.

The several SPOs also have their training that will follow the same general outline as the staff.

This is the recommended, up-front training package for all the participants. Later in the program, you will want to expand the training, especially for the staff, remembering that these are the people the company will promote to higher levels in the near future. The *Ned Hermann Brain Mapping Program, Situational Leadership, Targeted Selection, Managing Winning Proposals,* and a host of other training programs are desirable for selected people on the program.

Each level of kickoff for this program lasts all day. There are three levels of kickoff—SPO members to SPO leaders, staff to management, and staff to the customer. Before each of these meetings, have practices and dry runs. For a program of this size, this is not "gilding the lily," it is a necessity. The program is long and complex, and everyone must know their individual roles and the objectives of the team. Remember, the kickoff covers the Execution Stage and Closure. Everyone must agree on what constitutes closure, or you may as well not start.

The kickoff meeting should include a requirement for each presenter. The core team should indicate the contents of the presentation, the contributors (responsibilities), and the target audience for each presenter.

Execution Stage

The Execution Stage for a large-scale program is essentially the same as for a program, but the large-scale program is considerably larger and more complex. This is a good time to fine-tune your program plan.

The design period follows the same outline as did the program before. Because this is most likely a federal government contract, you will be confronted with a myriad of Mil Standards, Mil Specifications, and other required and specific documents, processes, and procedures. Each design review is conducted in strict accordance with MIL-STD-1521.[4] The chief engineer manages the reviews, but you must attend them all and be aware of all the details. Customer sign-off at all levels is essential for a program of this size.

The procurement period follows the same outline as the program did.

Each subsystem is developed on its own schedule. Indeed, some of the simpler subsystems can be completed far ahead of the others. It's your decision whether to proceed with all subsystems at once and put them into storage until the Final Integration Test (FIT) or to delay the start of each so that they all finish at the same time. Of course, there are advantages and disadvantages to each approach—that's why you get the big bucks!

Each subsystem program manager here is involved in a constant state of "work arounds." Whatever plan was established yesterday needs to be modified today because something "doesn't fit right." This period will try your SPO PM's problem-solving skills.

You and your chief engineer must stay on top of all these subsystem issues and project any impacts on FIT.

The testing period follows the same outline as all the previous projects and programs. It is very complex and very demanding.

Closure Stage

Other than the normal elements of closure, the closure of a program of this magnitude may well be different. If you have been able to create other programs as spin-offs, you will handle the people in one way. If not, you must handle them as if this is a normal, phased-down program. At this point, I hope you have learned all there is to learn about project and program management. From here you will either go on to another large-scale program or take over an operation or a division. Whatever it is, you need to get ready for the next one.

Notes

1. Benjamin Franklin, *Poor Richard's Almanack* (Mount Vernon, N.Y.: Pauper Press, 1983): 55.
2. A line from the Jabberwocky Bird—a mythical bird that flew backward just to see where he had been. Introduced in a song by Phil Harris on the "Phyllis' Boyfriend" show, October 17, 1948.
3. Charles Dickens, *A Tale of Two Cities*, opening line of Book 1, Chapter 1.
4. MIL-STD-1521 is just one of many hundreds of U.S. federal government standards that provide the strict guidelines for controlling activities on federal government contracts. MIL-STD-1521 controls design reviews.

CHAPTER 10

Are You Ready for the Next One?

Occasionally, you will be asked or directed to go to the next project or program before finishing the one you are currently working on. Don't lose the opportunity, but first, audit the program you are leaving and have someone of authority agree with the audit. If your replacement does not conduct the program as well as you did, you have a recognized condition of the program as you left it. It can save your reputation or your job. Conversely, if you are assigned to an ongoing project or program, it is a good idea to audit that project or program as soon as you arrive. Here we have the opposite case in terms of performance but the same case in terms of establishing a baseline. In the case of the ongoing project, it will be difficult to conduct the audit, but you should insist that it be performed anyway.

Legally, corporations are perpetual. And so it is with project and program managers. Each must be preparing for the next project or program and looking for the next promotion. In the case of a corporation, it will be preparing itself through proposals. In the case of a project manager, he will be preparing himself through knowledge, experience, and performance. Indeed, these factors will determine what your next project will be.

What Will the Next One Be?

The next project or program you will lead depends entirely on where you are now. Let's assume you're leading a small project. Look at Figure 10-1. It pulls together the path of progress through the project levels as a graphical representation of what we have talked about throughout the book. The boxes with the heavy lines indicate project or program

Figure 10-1. What is your next move?

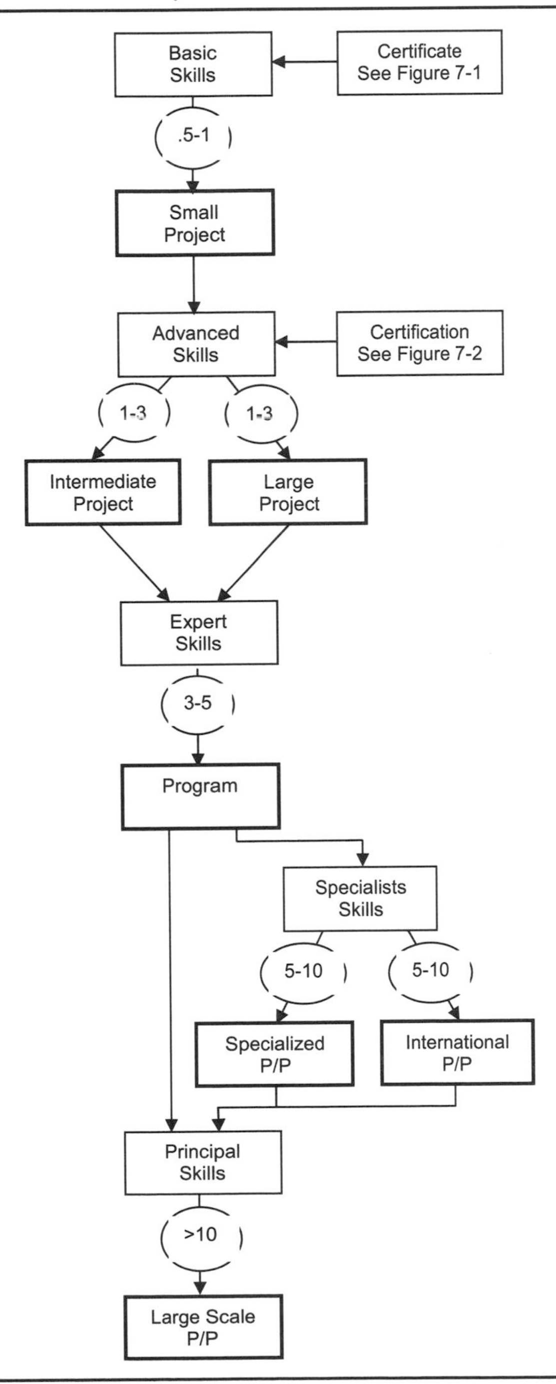

levels. The boxes with the normal lines indicate the skill levels. In between the boxes are circles containing numbers. These circles portray the experience, in years, required to move from one project or program level to another.

As you can see, an appropriate certificate can replace the Basic Skill Set requirements so long as the seminar offerings compare, at least, requirement to requirement.

Additionally, an appropriate certification can replace the Advanced Skill Set requirements so long as the certification courses compare, at least, requirement to requirement, and the candidate has the appropriate experience.

How Will You Get There?

Let's say you have entered the world of project management and have collected the skills necessary to lead a small project. In order to move up to an intermediate or large project, you must collect all the advanced skills necessary and have one to three years' experience at that level.

You can continue your progress through the project management ranks by gaining expert skills and three to five years' experience. Of course, a project or program must be available for you to lead when you are available. It is not unusual for a company to use a qualified project manager to lead or participate in a new business proposal whenever there is no immediate project to lead. This, of course, is a matter of chance and company practice. The bottom line is that you will either find project activity in your own company or move to another company.

Follow the same rationale to get you where you want to be. In fact, this scene will play over and over again throughout your project management career.

Depending on your education and training, you may have entered the "stream" somewhere other than at the small project level. In this case, only the entry point will be different. The rationale is the same from that point on.

PART V

MAKING YOUR CAREER MOVES

There are some jobs where you spend your entire career in the same position. For the most part, these positions are in mining and manufacturing. In most other industries, people move about from position to position and from company to company. This is certainly true in project management. The very nature of project management is that you must move from project to project because projects have a specific beginning and ending, they are finite.

The question in project management is not whether will you move, but how you will move. There are essentially four conditions to move through in the world of project management.

1. Move from project to project in the same company at the same level.
2. Move from project to project in the same company at different (higher) levels.
3. Move from project to project and from company to company at the same level.

4. Move from project to project and from company to company at different levels.

It is reasonable and normal to spend some amount of time in condition 1 above, but you want to move as quickly as you can from condition 1 to 2 or 4. You may have to move through condition 3 to get to condition 4.

First, you must look at your company's usual inventory of projects. Are they all at the same level or do the levels change? If they are all at the same level, that pretty much seals it. For all practical purposes, you will be working at that level at that company for the rest of your career. You will have traded your hardhat for a tie, but you are not much better off than the mine worker. If the projects change in size and nature, it's a different story. In this case, you must vie for a better position.

We spent much of the first four parts of this book suggesting that you improve yourself so that you could improve your position in project management and in the company. If someone doesn't move you, you need to move yourself. You do this by vying for higher positions in the company or by changing companies.

If other, higher positions are available in your company and you have increased your knowledge and performed well, you should be in position to be selected to lead other, higher projects. If you are not selected to lead other, higher projects, you need to know why. The amount of time you spend changing projects at the same level depends on three things. First, what is the duration of the project type you are working on? Some projects last for only a few months, while others last for several years. Second, what "mix" of project types does your company usually have—that is, how many short-duration projects does it have compared to how many long-duration projects? Third, how does your company reward the performance of project managers?

If other higher positions are not available and you have increased your knowledge and performed well, you need to seriously consider changing companies or at least divisions within your present company if jobs are available there. In any case, you need to make a move. The question is: Where and how do I move? Read on.

CHAPTER 11

Meeting Market Needs

Unfortunately we cannot individually create a market need for a position we would like to have. Instead, we must follow what the markets have to offer. We start the process by assessing the market. What are companies and other organizations looking for to fill their project management needs? We need to know if we are looking in the right places. What direction is the market taking? Who are the companies involved? What are the opportunities we might see in the market? What are the specific jobs being offered? Having digested all this, we need to address the market. That means we need to address the market with what it wants and needs. In other words, how we individually fit the needs of the market. We can set some strategies for ourselves in the process too. We can determine if we want to make the offered position a stopover or a destination, and most certainly we can take advantage of the different vista the new position provides.

Let's press on and capture that new job we want . . .

Assessing the Market

In part of the research I did for this book, I evaluated 182 current job postings for project managers. The results of the data showed that the most important requirement for all the project management jobs is a bachelor's degree. In some cases, the degree requirement was specific (engineering, finance, and so on). In other cases, it was general. At first I created a table to present the data, but the problem was that it was necessary to average the data. Why is this important? Because when you average data, you lose the individual characteristics of the elements of data. For instance, if a specific job posting is for a junior project manager, most likely the bachelor's degree and one to four years' experience will be most important. Conversely, if the job posting is for a senior-level program manager, the master's degree and ten to twenty years' experience will be most important. When the data is averaged, all this is lost. So, I decided I couldn't average the data. However, what came through loud and clear in all the postings was the requirement for a bachelor's degree. Experience was very important, but as you might expect, it was directly proportional to the expected compensation level of the job. In other words, the lower-level jobs required less experience than the higher-level jobs. Usually, the job experience requirement cut off at twenty years. Certification, per se, was rarely mentioned. Usually, if certification was required, the position was to be resold—that is, it was a headhunter posting the advertisement for the position, not the company. Performance was to be evaluated by the contents of the resume.

Market Direction

The direction of the project management market appears to follow general market trends with some exceptions. First, because project management is a new concept, there has been an avalanche of advertising for project managers in the last few years. In part, this advertisement is not so much the creation of new jobs as it is the reclassification of jobs to require the project management process be used in the performance of tasks that have been around for a long time. Second, because the project management process is so powerful, new jobs have been created requiring the use of the project management process. What all this means, though, is that you must have project management training in order to qualify for these jobs—existing or newly created.

Clearly, if the direction of the market is such that job descriptions now require project management abilities, you must have project management abilities. That's the basic point of this book.

The Companies Involved

The number and types of companies that advertise for project managers have increased dramatically in the last few years. This increase, however, follows the same rationale as addressed in direction, above.

Once this trend started, we began to see companies and industries advertising for project managers that have never advertised for project managers before. Examples are finance and banking, and believe it or not, construction. Before a few years ago, construction advertised for their traditional positions such as foreman and superintendent. Now, many companies advertise these positions as construction project managers. Depending on your view, you could say that this is subterfuge or that they should have been doing this all the time.

The Opportunities

The opportunities for project management positions appear both internally, meaning inside your current company (if your company does business using projects), and externally, meaning outside your current company. The process you use to achieve these positions is essentially the same.

Now, let me throw something at you. Outsourcing has had a severe impact on America's workforce. Jobs, at all levels, are being sent overseas. Manufacturing jobs, software coding jobs, analyst jobs, white-collar jobs of all types. White-collar jobs, EXCEPT project management jobs. Why is that? Because the project management process provides leverage in getting the job done, and that's what's needed here.

What does this mean to you? It means you need to get your start in project management before your competition does. Secure your position by becoming qualified in project management.

Job Descriptions

In Chapter 7, I talked about the value of certification. Here is where you need to make an individual assessment based on the market you are working in. Let's look at the issue from two positions:

Position 1. Look at a number of job descriptions (meaning as many as you can find) for positions you would like to have. Has the market segment you are looking into started requiring certifications? How many of them are requiring certifications? If the number is 10 percent or more that are requiring certifications, perhaps this is a portent of things to come. You need to think about a year or two ahead. That's the length of time it will take you to become certified. Can you visualize how many companies in your area of interest will be requiring certifications at that time?

If your market segment approaches that 10 percent threshold at the present time, you need to seriously think about getting a certification.

Position 2. Remember when I discussed the two project managers with exactly the same qualifications, except that one has a certification and the other does not? Remember the obvious conclusion we came to? Apply that logic and increase your competitive position by getting a certification. Which certification you choose is a matter of the demands of the market you are working in.

Addressing the Market

Where to go from here is a question you must ask yourself. In previous chapters, I provided some information that hopefully has stimulated your imagination, and you now have a better idea of where you want to go or what you want to do in the field of project management. At this point, consider three options: First, evaluate this position in light of your overall strategy, then ask yourself: Is this a stopover or a destination? Second, evaluate the visibility that this position affords you with regard to your overall strategy, then ask yourself: Do I have a different view from here? Finally, if you have decided that your present position is not your final destination and your visibility tells you there are bigger and better things out there, then ask yourself: Where do I look?

Is This a Stopover or a Destination?

Maybe you are now in a position to determine whether the next position you take will be a stopover or a destination. In either case, it is your choice. Hopefully you will make the choice before you take the next position, but that's not entirely necessary. On the one hand, what started out as a stopover could end up being a destination. If you are satisfied with the position you are going into, that's wonderful. On the other hand, if a position starts out as a destination and then you find other opportunities available, that's terrific.

All this may sound kind of wishy-washy, but it's really not. At the outset, you should develop a strategy built on the view you now have. At this point you say: "I want to be a project vice president, and any job is just a stopover on my way to getting there." At the next vantage point you have a different view. You see that staying close to your technical roots is more promising in the long run. If that's the case, shift your strategy a little and take a slightly different vector. When you get to the next vantage point, do the same thing. The point is this, have a good idea of what you want to do and maintain the general strategy. Don't make sharp right or left turns on a whim. Usually, these look real good, but don't pan out too well. Maintain the general course, but don't be afraid to take advantage of a new offering.

Do You Have a Different View from Here?

Each position you get will likely give you a different view. You are exposed to different people who have different views. These people may have other contacts and friends in places and positions you had not thought of before. Every day, indeed every cocktail party, every golf match, or every little league game, can offer new opportunities. Just keep your career and your career strategy in mind at all times and keep your eyes and your mind open.

Where Do You Look?

Before we tackle the "where" question, let's tackle the "how" question. The answer to "how" is networking. Networking takes two forms: Face-to-face networking and remote networking.

Face-to-face networking is the kind of networking you can accomplish by going to the social activities that your company offers and interfacing with section heads, managers, and directors of other parts of the company that might be interested in what you have to offer. The point is to use this forum to break the ice and set up a follow-on meeting so you can get down to business. I don't suggest you bring your resume with you to the party, but cards are OK.

Remote networking is accomplished by letter, fax, e-mail, and telephone with companies and people of common interest. You can start remote networking by joining a technical organization, an administrative organization, a management organization, or a project management organization. Almost all of these organizations have bulletin boards, potential employers lists, and numerous other kinds of contacts to get you started. Because the lists are so dynamic, many organizations have Web sites where these lists are posted. The thing you have in common with these kinds of interchanges is that you both have a common interest in the organization that brought you together in the first place. You will need to provide your credentials, your resume, and the other standard documents you usually provide, but you should be able to break the ice with your contacts by referring to the organization that provided the contact in the first place.

Now that we understand the "how," let's look at the "where."

Project Management Organizations. You are looking at an organization to provide you with educational opportunities, training opportunities, book lists, listings of gatherings (seminars and such), networking opportunities, and most importantly, a job listing board where you can post your resume or look at the listings for opportunities.

Figure 2-2 lists organizational contacts no matter what continent you are standing on. Take the opportunity to contact the organization that interests you most and see what they have to offer. I believe this is good advice if you are a "newbie" or a "grizzly." If you are a newbie, the organization can provide you with mounds of information to help you in many ways. If you are a grizzly, take a moment to stick your head above the trenches and see what is happening in the outside world. I guarantee you will be amazed. In either case, you will have the opportunities to see jobs posted or to post your resume.

Most organizations have Special Interest Groups (they may call them something else that is similar) that allow you to channel your interests into a specific discipline, industry, or area. The main body provides the standards and the body of knowledge for general project management positions, but the Special Interest Group (SIG) provides a specific interest flair. Most of these organizations have local chapters. You may need to drive a few miles every few months to reach the meeting place, but believe me, it's worth the effort. These organizations usually have a guest speaker who presents a topic of interest during the meeting. Usually, there is a "networking" period prior to the meeting, so you can move around and meet others. My experience with these local chapters has been excellent. The groups are populated by project managers and potential project managers from all the local industries. They usually run the gamut in age and the industry in which they are employed. The local dues are usually low, and the return on investment in time and money are more than worth it.

Civic Organizations. Next, you can join organizations that stimulate interchange between members. The Chamber of Commerce is a good place to look for organizations of this type. Most of these organizations will have a social hour or period for interfacing that will be of immense value to you. Once again, this is an initial contact situation. Business cards or personal cards are a good way to suggest maintaining contact. Don't give out a card to everyone you see, but have some in your pocket just in case. Then, just handle the situation as if it's no big deal.

Job Fairs. In addition to these types of face-to-face interchanges, there are job fairs and expos. Even though job fairs and expos offer face-to-face contact, they are a little different. The usual setup for these events is to have the company representatives at tables around the room. The representatives will be standing at some kind of "parade rest" behind their table wearing a big smile. There must be only one training school in the world for these folks, because this is the way it always happens. You circulate until something or someone catches your eye, then you swoop (no, you'd better be cool and saunter) over to that table. After about five seconds of pleasantries, you get down to business. The purpose of this interchange is simple—what can you offer me, and what can I offer you? Does this sound like a marriage made in heaven? Oh well, probably not, but it may be a good contact. Answer the representative's questions and ask your own. Be sure to have a good supply of up-to-date resumes and personal or business cards. If you don't know how to write a resume, get help. Read a book or contact a professional service. There's a myriad of books and hundreds if not thousands of resume services to help you, all for a fee, of course. Why? Because just after you turn and leave the smiling representative at the table, your resume goes into a pile, maybe with a few notes but nevertheless into a pile. The next time it is read, you won't be there to defend it, and it may end up in the trash. At this point, the face-to-face networking has turned into remote networking.

Classified Ads. The most difficult way to get a job is through "cold calling." Sometimes this is the only way open to you, but it's tough. By cold calling, I mean looking in the newspaper or the like and trying to respond to a job posting. They don't know you from Adam's house cat, and you are just another piece of paper. Unless you have some unique qualification they happen to be looking for at that moment in time, you will spend a lot of unproductive, frustrating time pursuing this avenue. The only time this method is really useful is when it is a seller's market and employers are hiring everyone they can get.

So, choose your method. I think the priority of choice should be clear from the foregoing. Always have an updated resume available, and always carry business or personal cards, along with a smile!

CHAPTER 12

Getting Settled

Assume you made the decision to change, meaning you were hired into a new company or were transferred from one group to another within the company you are in. For whatever reason, your situation today is not what it was yesterday. This means you have to make a change in yourself. You must be in charge and must show your leadership style from the very outset.

To start, get a sense of the big picture, the lay of the land. First, you should fully understand the organization—this means the company organization and the project organization. The best way I know to get an overview of the formal organization is to ask for an organization chart. Then, you need to understand your bosses. Do your homework and find out just what kind of people they are. What are their likes and dislikes? What are their other personal traits? Only when you know all these things can you approach your boss with an issue and get something done. Next comes the power structure. Who drives the organization? Sometimes the answer to this question is surprising. Next make friends and alliances—you need them in order to get your job done. Finally, you are ready to take over the project you will lead. How do you do that to ensure you are leading the project to success from the very first moment? This chapter tells you how and makes some real suggestions to get the job done.

Getting the Lay of the Land

Getting the lay of the land means understanding the company, the unit, the products, the project, and the people. What about the attitude of the people in the company? Are they all working together or are there self-serving cliques? Were you immediately treated as one of the family or have you had to earn your way? Will you be accepted or will you forever be the guy from somewhere else? Every company is different, and each has its own character and its own idiosyncrasies. You must understand the character or you will forever play "What happened?" I remember when I moved from New Hampshire to Houston, I immediately became one of the family. This mainly had to do with my technical expertise, but it also had to do with the people. The people were, by nature, open and friendly, but the most important factor was that the program was brand-new, and everybody had come from somewhere else. There was no organizational inertia to overcome. However, when I moved from Houston to Philadelphia, it was another story. Philadelphia was the headquarters for the company I worked for, and most of the people there had always been there. "Always" is not an exaggeration. Some had been there for thirty-five years and more. I was treated as an outsider, but then again, so was everyone else who had moved in from the field. Over time I made peace with the technical and management staff, but I was never fully accepted by most of the clerical staff. They were as polite as they had to be, but there was always an undertone of having the lowest priority for my clerical work. You can fight this kind of situation if you want to, but have you ever heard the expression "pushing a wet rope uphill?" That's about the size of it. If you can't convert the entire workforce, get enough people on your side to get the work done. Understand who has the ability to expedite work, and, conversely, who can hold it up. Griping about the situation won't help. Frequently, a lunch or two with the right people will help. It is amazing how people take on a different mantle when they are in a group of "their own" but become affable when you meet with them on an individual basis. If you handle these one-on-one situations diplomatically, these folks will frequently take your message back to "their own," and you will become more and more accepted.

These are the kinds of things you may be exposed to whenever you move to a new location. I can only suggest that you start with diplomacy. It's easiest to start as a diplomat and then lapse into your street-fighting mode if necessary. But, once you expose your street-fighting side, that's where you'll stay. The higher the level you are hired or transferred to in an organization, the fewer of these kinds of problems you can expect to have. But, even then, there's no guarantee. Some of it relates to the environment, and some of it relates to you. In addition to learning about the general organization, do your homework, and discover everything you can about your new bosses, not to be nosy, but to be more effective. If you take a problem to your boss, how should you present it? Should you ever take a problem to your boss? As silly as this may sound, you may get a response you didn't expect. Perhaps the response is "Don't bring me problems, bring me results." This may be because your boss wants to train you to solve your own problems; it may be because he or she is too lazy to be bothered. You need to know. Perhaps the response is something you did not expect—a total whirlwind. You've turned the machine on, and now you can't turn it off. It's out of control—most certainly it's out of your control. Don't get caught in this kind of situation. Your boss may hand you a solution you can't live with! Furthermore, your boss will then expect you to implement his or her solution, and be in your stuff at every turn until you do. It is best to go in with your own solution and give your boss the opportunity to say: "Yes." That's the easiest solution, and the one they normally take.

Before you make your next move, get a copy of *Games People* Play,[1] and understand that different people have different games they play. To understand that you are in the middle of a game—and that it has a name—is halfway to fixing the problem.

The Organization

What is the company organization, and what is its character? What is the source of project personnel? Will your people be provided through a matrix organization, or is your project "projectized?" To whom do you report functionally? Is there a "dotted line" reporting scheme? Is there a centralized Project Management Office (PMO), or are the projects on their own?

Phew! That's a bunch of questions, and the answer to each is important. Let's take a look at each one.

What is the company organization and character? Is the company a Research and Development (R&D) organization? Is the company a manufacturing organization? Is the company a services organization? Is the company a hardware-oriented organization? Is the company a software organization? I don't mean to answer a question with other questions, but these distinctions are important. Each organization type has its own character, and you must understand what that character is. If all your experience has been in manufacturing and you are going into an R&D organization, you will find the character of the two quite different. I've only presented two company types for purposes of explanation. There are, of course, many other types, and you need to be aware of what you are getting into. Sometimes, the purpose of the organization is not consistent with the usual character of the organization type. For instance, early in my career, I hired into an R&D organization. It seemed reasonable to expect an R&D atmosphere, right? Well, it may have been reasonable to expect that atmosphere, but that's not what it was. This organization was a spin-off of an old-time manufacturing organization, and they carried their manufacturing rules and policies with them when they founded this new R&D arm. There was difficulty in the organization from day one, and it continued for as long as I was there. It's one of the main reasons I left. Some time later, the organization changed, but only after there was a change in upper management resulting in a change in management philosophy. Look at the organization you are going into and understand its expectations. For instance, if your new organization is an old-line manufacturing organization, expect the procedures to be solid. You will need to conform to the mold. The emphasis is on production, even for the projects. If your new organization is a new software house, expect a lot of serendipity and few procedures. The emphasis will be on creativity. Over time, this attitude will change . . . if the company survives.

How does your new organization provide the personnel to the projects? Will your project be a matrix, or is it "projectized?" To recap the operating characteristics of a matrix organization, let me say that a project operating under the matrix concept gets its personnel from functional organizations. These personnel get their raises from their functional managers and thus owe their allegiance to the functional manager. What does this mean to you? Simply stated, you are required to provide more leadership and fewer orders to get the project personnel to do what you need them to do. Some "enlightened" organizations (where the higher management has been a project manager) institute a process that allows the project manager to have a heavy input to the individual's performance evaluations. This action gives the project manager a lot more leverage in the individual's performance appraisal, meaning his raises!

On the other hand, if your project is projectized, you have considerably direct control because you are the one who passes out the raises and promotions. You can expect responsiveness to be a lot more crisp.

To whom do you report functionally? This means purely and simply, who signs your paycheck, your promotions, and your raises? Is there a "dotted line" reporting relationship? A dotted line simply means this is the office that coordinates and may temporarily control your operating activities. Is there a straight line and a dotted line to your function? If this is the case, you report functionally to one office and are technically directed by another office. This is usual for quality assurance people and is used with project managers whenever the centralized PMO staff concept is used (see below).

Is the Project Management Office (PMO) a LINE function or a

STAFF function? The PMO usually has one of two functions. If it is a LINE organization, it is the organization element from which all project management activities emanate. In this case, the PMO is the directing agency for all project activities in the company. It is the creator of all project management policies, plans, processes, and procedures. It is the "home" or functional organization of all project managers. It makes assignments and controls the activities of project managers to each project. The line PMO controls the raises of the project managers.

Alternatively, it can be a STAFF organization from which project management activities are coordinated. In this case, it is the creator or coordinator of project management policies, plans, processes, and procedures. It "logs" projects and may receive reports from ongoing projects. In some cases, the PMO will simply collect and post project performance data. But, the project managers do *not* report functionally to this PMO; instead, they are technically responsible to the PMO for employing the policies, plans, and procedures demanded by the PMO but functionally responsible to their line functional manager or director. The functional manager, in this case, controls the project manager raises.

What does all this mean to you? It means you need to understand the position and authority from which you operate whenever you go into a new organization. You should know who signs your paycheck and who signs the paychecks of the people on your team. You should know the method of control you have over the personnel on your project. You must know to whom you report and in what capacity. By knowing all these things, your assimilation into the new organization will be a lot easier.

The Power Structure

There are frequently two elements of the power structure in any organization. These elements are the organizational structure, reflected by the organization chart hanging on the wall and the infrastructure that is never written down.

Ostensibly, the organization chart reflects the power structure of the organization it represents. The closer one is to the top, the more power he or she has. Power, usually meaning the ability to give orders, is directed downward. However, in many organizations, the power structure is not the same as the organizational structure. Indeed, it is sometimes amazing to see who in the organization has the true control of what goes on.

The infrastructure is a loosely gathered network of people involved in information and activity flow. It is always interesting to find who the king or queen of this network is. Frequently, the person resides among the secretaries and the clerks. But be careful. If you listen to this network, you must also have a "rumor filter." You must be able to filter out what is rumor and what is fact. Over time, you will be able to distinguish between those who think they know what's going on and those who really do.

All these things create the organizational dynamic, and you must learn what makes the dynamic move and get things done. If you don't understand the dynamic, you will be treading water while others are succeeding. Every good project manager keeps his or her finger on the pulse of both the organizational structure and the infrastructure.

These things are very subtle. As I mentioned in the story about going to headquarters earlier in this chapter, the power structure can be among the clerical staff. Do they give the orders? No, but they do control work flow and who gets what and when. You are either in or out. Sometimes you may be tolerated. Can you do anything about it? Let me tell you a story that circulated about Lyndon Johnson when he became president of the United States. On his way up, some functionary in the Interior Department made a change to the application of policy that radically affected his ranch in Texas. Johnson was furious. Some months after he became president, one of his friends asked: "Did you fire that guy?" Johnson answered, "Fire him? I couldn't even find the SOB." That's the way a lot of these things are—very subtle.

In addition to the organizational dynamic, you must also understand the organizational culture. In a new organization, the culture will reflect the desires of the leader. In an old-line organization, the culture will reflect a conglomerate of the desires of all the past leaders of the organization and, to some extent, the people of the organization.

Even the culture of an old-line organization can be changed by a dynamic leader, at least temporarily. When a new general manager, CEO, or other "top dog" comes into an organization, it is normal for that person to demand the organization follow his or her dictates. Depending on the leadership and time of tenure, the culture of an organization may be changed. On the other hand, the inherent strength of the culture may render the new "leader" ineffective or it may return to its roots as soon as this person goes away.

What does all this mean to you? Simply that you must keep your eyes and ears open when going into a new organization. You can read and understand the organizational policies and procedures, but you must discover the organization's dynamic and its culture. If you don't, you are in for a lot of frustration.

Making Friends and Alliances

If you are hired for or assigned to an ongoing project, the best advice I can offer is to first conduct an audit of the project. The audit should at least cover scope, budget, schedule, and customer opinion. Determine if there are any specific issues plaguing the project and who or what has been involved with these issues. Document your findings. The thing you want to do is to establish a starting point from which you are considered responsible. Whether or not you present these findings to your management is a political choice. You must make that judgment.

When you move into a new position, you need to do two things: listen and exhibit confidence. By listening, I mean just that. Talk to those who have been with the project for a while and understand the dynamic of the project and its strengths and weaknesses. You are likely to get some conflicting views, so be careful in sorting out the data. By confidence, I don't mean cockiness, I mean confidence. You get confidence by knowledge and performance. You must understand what your new position is all about and then apply your past knowledge and experience to that situation. Once you have a good feel for that, you should look for alliances to establish. Hopefully, you have been there for a few days and have had your eyes open to see who knows what and who claims they do. They most certainly fall into two different piles, and you must be able to separate them. Your purpose in making friends and alliances is to get the job done. If you are at a high enough level, you may bring some staff with you. However, unless you are at the director level or above, you are probably on your own. Remember, whenever you select your friends and alliances to be a part of your team or to support your team, you are not selecting someone to drink beer with. You are selecting people that will make or break your project and your career by their performance. Select them carefully.

Before you start to select your people and make allies, keep your eyes open for high performers to create a core team. Once you have confidence in a core team and they in you, start selecting the next levels of people for your team. Consider group interviewing using the Targeted Selection Process. The core team members will have been there for a while and will have more insight into who are the performers and who are not. This strategy just makes your initial job easier. Now you only need to select a few key people, and they will help you fill out the team.

It is usually a good idea to work with your core team and to keep the project team member selection confidential until the time is right to make the information public. At this time, all the kinks regarding proficiency and availability have been worked out and your selection process appears to be smooth and complete. For your first team selection, it is not unusual to conduct interviews with the potential team members, much as you would if you were hiring them. All this presumes you have the latitude to make these selections. Interestingly, even though you may not have been told you have this latitude, you can discuss it with your boss. I did this once, and the reason I had not been given that latitude is that no one thought of it before. When I discussed it with my new boss, he agreed, and away we went. Of course you need to read your new boss. It's a good idea to do your homework and find out the nature of your new boss before taking on a position. He or she can just as easily hand you your head as agree with you.

Taking Over a Project

The first question to be answered is: Why are you here? Were you hired to take over and lead this project? Were you moved into a position to take over this project? No matter which question you answered, the first thing you need to do is to get your act together. By this I mean, when you walk into the project, walk in as the project manager, not as someone looking for friends. In other words, walk in strong, not weak.

Have you gone through all the prior steps of this chapter? Do you understand the organization? Have you made the alliances you need to make? If you are coming in from the outside, make these steps carefully. Get answers to these questions by talking to your trusted contacts inside the organization or to the person who hired you. If you are already in the organization, you may already have a feel for these situations. The point is, get the questions answered and the issues resolved at the outset.

First, what are the conditions you are looking into as a project manager? There are usually six combinations:

You are hired for a new project.
You are transferred for a new project.
You are hired for an ongoing project that is running well.
You are transferred to an ongoing project that is running well.
You are hired for an ongoing project that is in trouble.
You are transferred to an ongoing project that is in trouble.

It is important to understand which of these conditions you are facing. Hopefully, you had an opportunity to find out the condition of the project before taking the job, but this does not always happen. No matter what, you must still get your arms around the situation before going any further. In the above list, it is clear that the first four situations are the best and the easiest to tackle. The last two situations are more difficult.

You have just been hired or transferred to take over the project. Has there been a problem? What was the problem? Listen to the people who are already there. Likely they will have some insightful ideas of what the problem is all about. Be very careful in your assessment of each individual input. Audit the inputs and the project performance figures and derive your own solution. What is the solution, and how will you implement it? Will you make organization changes? Will you make changes to the order of work? This is the time to broach all these questions (and any others that may be appropriate) and have your answers ready. Modify the project plan so that your approach is documented. Then, present the changes to the team. Nothing makes an organization understand that you are in charge more than making organizational and procedural changes, but they must be the right ones.

When you are ready, call the team together and make your presentation. It is not necessary to be gruff or unfriendly, but you do need to let the team members understand you are in charge. You don't ever say that, you do that by having your act together. Don't make your presentation with a strong voice, make it with a strong plan. Of course the antithesis of this is to be placed in a position where you have no time to prepare. Don't let that happen. Even if it's just overnight, be prepared to take over.

The adage "You never get a second chance to make a first impression" is absolutely true. Be ready to make that first impression, and make it with positive strength.

Up until now, you have been getting ready. You looked at the origins and development of project management. You looked at your background and where you wanted to go. You put the two together, and you were hired or moved into getting a position to lead a project. Now it's time to get serious in leading the project or program, but first you need to know what each classification is all about. Are you going to be a one-person project manager? Are you going to lead a project or a program, or are you going to lead a large-scale project or program? These are all valid questions and must be answered.

Note

1. Eric Berne, M.D., *Games People Play* (New York: Ballantine Books, 1996).

PART VI

KEEP THE MOMENTUM GOING

The traditional way to end a book is to provide a summary of what was presented and to draw the process to an end. But here success is the process, and success has no end. It is much more descriptive to think of success as a continuum, and you are now at a point on that continuum.

Hopefully, you have followed the advice of the book and have raised your career to new levels, and you are now at an advanced point on the continuum.

At the outset of the book, I said: "Project management is a dynamic discipline, and you really need to stay on top of it. New ideas, new software, and new approaches are being developed every day." Your task is to keep the momentum going and to continually move all the factors now in your possession along the continuum.

This is the place in your career where you can apply your skills not only to your job, but also to other activities and continue your success. Your new and well-earned reputation will be the spear point that leads the way.

You are now at a point where you can give back more than your labor. You can contribute to the organization of which you are a part.

You can contribute to the discipline in which you operate. You can contribute to the community in which you live.

Continue your success by availing yourself of the latest ideas in every discipline applicable to project management. History, psychology, mathematics, and social studies are all applicable. Indeed, what is not applicable?

CHAPTER 13

Applying Your Skills to Other Activities

As your project management career progresses, you will become more and more valuable to yourself and to your company. It is to your advantage and to the advantage of your company to share your skills with others and to lead other tasks within the company. This readily becomes a positively reinforced process. By being more valuable to the company, you are more valuable to yourself, and so on.

You are in a position now to add breadth and depth to the knowledge base for project management used in your company and perhaps the organizations to which you belong. Searching for new ideas applicable to project management is high on the list of how you can apply your knowledge and expertise. The application of your project management skills may be in mentoring less experienced project managers. Mentoring is also applicable to others who are not project managers, such as administrative people and technical people. Many projects need administrators knowledgeable in project management techniques, while other projects need technical people knowledgeable in project management techniques. It will be your pleasure to apprise them of these techniques.

At this level, you can be the architect for developing a project management office (PMO) within your company, you can be the catalyst for new ideas for managing projects using the standards now available through your participation in project management organizations, and you can chair project activities within your company.

Now is the time to share what you have gained—to give back some of what you have learned.

Gathering Leading-Edge Ideas

As you progressed through the skill sets, I'm sure you saw that the subjects were not only getting deeper, they were getting broader as well. At this point, breadth and depth are infinite.

There are many experts in project management who are advancing the field. But there are also experts in other fields, such as mathematics, psychology, and sociology, who have ideas that are applicable to our field. There are good ideas in places we never dreamed that could contribute to our discipline. Now, you have the visibility that can make far-reaching contributions to project management in your company and perhaps in other places as well.

At this point, it is imperative that you keep up with what's going on around you. Your attention should be drawn to reading such books as *Rethinking the Future* by Rowan Gibson, Alvin Toffler, and Heidi Toffler and *The Strategy-Focused Organization* by Robert S. Kaplan and David P. Norton. You should attend such seminars as *Developing and Executing a Customer-Centric Strategy* and question the application of Knowledge Management to what's going on in your organization. By all means these are not the only areas you should investigate; these are presented here just to give some idea of the kinds of directions your interests may take at this point.

At the outset of this book and many times later, I said that project management is an evolving discipline. It is not today what it was yesterday, and it will not be tomorrow what it is today. The evolution comes from leading-edge ideas. At first, these ideas are "soft"; that is, they are conceptual. As they grow and evolve, however, they become more "firm."

Mentoring and Training

To be called upon, either by management or by another project manager, to be a mentor means that you are considered expert enough to train others. It means that your abilities are well-respected and valuable.

Mentoring, believe it or not, is a two-way street—that is, you get as much from mentoring as your students do. You get to formalize and solidify your knowledge and experience. You will discover things you didn't even know you knew. You will find things you knew but had forgotten the details of and needed to research to bring yourself back up to speed.

You will gain knowledge from your students. They will be thinking from another frame of reference and bringing experiences and knowledge to the meetings that are new to you. Likely they will be younger than you. By being younger, they will have a different view of things. If you listen, as well as talk, you will learn something.

Policies, Processes, Plans, and Procedures

Now it is your turn to change and update the policies, processes, plans, and procedures you've been griping about for the last number of years. Two things will come to the fore here. First, you will probably find that many of the policies, processes, and so on were not so bad after all, now that you understand them from a senior management viewpoint. Second, you will have an opportunity to fine-tune them with the knowledge and the experience base you have created for yourself over the last few years.

A Project Management Office?

Does your organization have a project management office? Does it need one? Does the one it has need changing? Now, as a senior project manager, you will have the opportunity to be heard on the subject. You may want to tackle the book *The Advanced Project Management Office* by Parvis Rad and Ginger Levin and apply some of the appropriate tricks the author talks about. Some of the best program-oriented companies in the world use the PMO concept. The concept keeps IBM on the straight and narrow, and it helped Federal Express turn around.

If you don't want or can't afford a PMO office, how about a project management executive committee; an ad hoc group specializing in best practices of project management and flowing these ideas through the organization? The group can have a yearly conclave with an inspirational speaker to rev up the troops and send them on their way for the next year. A panel can present the findings of their research. Awards and recognition can be given at the annual meeting. The meeting will follow the same format as a marketing and sales meeting. To do the job we have to do, we need to be pumped too. We need to be inspired and need to take away new ideas from the conclave. And, probably most important of all, we need to meet new project and program managers; get to know their capabilities and personalities, and see their awards; and see what it takes to make it to the top in this company and in project management as a whole.

Suggested Reading

Gibson, Rowan (ed.), Alvin Toffler, and Heidi Toffler. *Rethinking the Future: Rethinking Business, Principles, Competition, Control & Complexity, Leadership, Markets, and the World.* New York: Nicholas Brealey, 1999.

Kaplan, Robert S., and David P. Norton. *The Strategy-Focused Organization.* Boston: Harvard Business School Press, 2001.

Rad, Parvis, and Ginger Levin. *The Advanced Project Management Office.* New York: CRC Press, 2002.

Seminars

Developing and Executing a Customer-Centric Strategy
See: http://www.amanet.org/seminars/cmd2/2585.htm

CHAPTER 14

Continuing Your Success!

Once you enter the success continuum, you will want to continue on and on, broader and broader, and higher and higher.

Continuing success in project management is a matter of conjoining the two most cogent facts of this book. First, recognizing that project management is a growing, evolving discipline. Second, that the path to success really is: **Knowledge + Experience + Persona × Performance**.

When you started this book, where did you find yourself? Were you at the beginning? Were you somewhere in the middle? Did you assess your capabilities along the way so you could have a baseline for improvement? Did that tell you anything about yourself? Where are you now? Will you continue to assess yourself throughout your career? No, this is not a test. It is simply an assessment of the book as it applies to you and an assessment of you as you apply to the continuum of project management learning.

We started this book with some pretty basic stuff. I described what project management is all about, who and what a project manager is, and the project management process, and then introduced the path to success. Then, I introduced the principal organizations, the differences between them, and the commonalities they shared.

In this book, you were introduced to project and program types, to project and program skill sets, and then to the differences between leadership roles. Then you saw how the skill sets were used in leading the different project and program types. What came through was that each skill set and each project type was more involved than the previous one and that they were all linked together. They were part of a continuum.

Then, you learned the language, as it applies to this book, and with an understanding that each organization and each industry has its own language. There is a move to commonality, but we are not there yet.

What about the project management skills presented in Part II? Did you see yourself here? Are you planning to expand your knowledge? Are you planning to gain more experience? What about developing your persona? Is that a worthwhile thing for you to do?

I presented a lot of references to books and seminars and courses and threw a lot of ideas on the table. I hope one thing is clear, though, and that is that your success is up to your performance. You can read all the books, attend all the seminars, and lead some projects, but if the projects are not successful, you will not have success. This all boils down to the fact that success is really up to you.

But, I believe, if you've had the stick-to-it-iveness to do all these things, and reach this point in the book, you will succeed.

I hope, after reading this book, you found that you need to:

1. Get the best education and the highest you can get by choosing the best curriculum and the best college available to you.
2. Get the most training you can get by choosing the appropriate seminars and workshops that will provide you with the most information.
3. Get the best experience in the proper order that will allow you to grow to greater and greater heights in your project management performance.
4. Join a professional organization that will provide you with opportunities to network and to look for job opportunities as well as extending your training.
5. Get a certification and certificates to enhance your background.
6. Keep a positive mental attitude in your education, training, and performance at every level.
7. Constantly strive to perform the best you possibly can for the sake of your project, your company, and yourself and work every job every day of your professional career as if your reputation depends on it—because it most certainly does!

Finally, remember that project management is evolving, and you must evolve with it. You must continue with your education and training. You must apply what you know and gain experience in the real world. You must present yourself as a leader and as a winner. And, most of all, you must show positive performance in all that you do. At this point you will have applied all the elements of the formula for success and can enjoy:

YOUR SUCCESSFUL PROJECT MANAGEMENT CAREER

Glossary

After Receipt of Order (ARO) A number, usually expressed in days, weeks, or months, as a point after the official notification of the start of the project. Example: The PDR is due 90 days ARO. This technique allows the elements of a project schedule to move relative to the award or beginning of a project or program.

AID The Agency for International Development. Also USAID or U.S. Agency for International Development. An independent federal government agency that supports low-term and equitable economic growth, and advances U.S. foreign policy objectives.

Alliance A grouping of two or more companies for one project or program (a tactical alliance) or for all projects or programs (strategic alliance) that require a particular combination of products or services.

Architecture The structure established for the system as a whole or the structure established for a subsystem within the system.

Arm's Length A legitimate deal, open for view.

Assertion An affirmative statement.

Award Fee (AF) A fee arrangement where fee payment is based on some predetermined factors such as schedule, quality, and cost performance. Usually awarded unilaterally by the customer.

Balanced Scorecard A complex process that ties four distinct perspectives to strategies that drive and measure performance.

Benchmark Also referred to as Best Practices, Exemplary Practices, and Business Excellence. Usually a series of studies regarding business processes and practices among businesses in the same or sometimes disparate business areas. One can use the benchmarks to compare their performance to others. The benchmarks may or may not be the best measure of excellence.

Best and Final The absolute last opportunity to submit your most favorable position.

Best-of-Breed A term applied to a system or process that has singular or limited application but is the best there is for that application. The highest level of achievement for that element.

Boilerplate Standard terminology, paragraph, page, or section used in all documents of the same type.

Brainstorming Method A method used to get every conceivable input from all participants. Usually conducted in a classroom environment with all attendees' participation. The idea is to get as much input as possible and then go back and eliminate, by consensus, those duplicated inputs and those that have no validity.

Brassboard Similar to **Breadboard** (see below) but usually with hard parts that are soldered or welded together. Not a deliverable.

Breadboard A table layout of the article being developed so that parts and wiring can be changed easily. Breadboards are usually many times the physical size of the final product. Not a deliverable.

Budget Review A review of the budget associated with all or part of a task or contract. Usually, but not always, budget reviews are conducted concurrently with schedule reviews and performance reviews in project, program, or division reviews.

Business Factors Having to do with the processes necessary to achieve and maintain business. May include the Research and Development (R&D) processes and the proposal processes.

Business Process Improvement A generalized term that includes such specific programs as Total Quality Management (TQM), Business Process Reengineering (BPR), Benchmarking, and Best Practices, as well as other less well-known programs aimed at improving the process of a business.

Buying In The act of bidding a project or program at cost or less than cost for any number of reasons.

Capability Matrix A matrix consisting of tasks up the side and previous projects across the top. An intersect is acknowledged whenever the project contained the task and was successfully completed. The purpose of the capability matrix is to determine whether or not to bid a program or to identify those capabilities in inventory and those needed to approach a program or project.

Capability Maturity Model (CMM) A model for judging the maturity of the software processes of an organization and for identifying the key practices that are required to increase the maturity of these processes.

Cellar Agency A government agency that is not known to the public and may not be known to anyone outside a carefully controlled ring of cleared persons.

Challenge (Tasking) A top-down application of budget and/or schedule and/or manpower that is less than requested. The Challenge (tasking) imposed upon a **Work Package** leader by the **Project Office** (project manager).

Change Order (CO) A formal change introduced into a project controlled by a Change Management process.

Chomping at the Bit Anxious to get started.

Column of Mobs An old Army expression indicating that the situation is total chaos.

Communication Meetings, reports, and verbal transfers between team members, between the team and the customer, and between the team and its subcontractors and other providers.

Company A corporation or partnership.

Contract Data Requirements List (CDRL) A list of documents that are contractually deliverable under the terms of a contract.

Contract Line Item Number (CLIN) An ordering or sequencing number assigned to functional or physical deliverables that are contractually required on a program.

CONUS Continental United States.

Core Team The management element of the team usually consisting of the project manager, the chief engineer, and others of the same ilk.

Corporation A legal entity composed of a number of people joined together for a common purpose. Such legal entities are formed under local, state, or federal laws. Some are public corporations, and some are private corporations. Some private corporations are organized for profit, and some are organized for nonprofit. Public corporations often issue stock to their owners in return for the money they invest.

Cost The direct cost of labor or the labor hours used on your project. Depending on your company financial procedures, it may include benefits, overhead, and **General and Administrative (G&A)** costs.

Cost of Quality A cost factor added to the basic bid cost by a subcontractor for labor and materials to bring the subcontractor's product up to the quality he should have produced, but didn't. The Cost of Quality is a consideration when evaluating bids by subcontractors. The amount bid by a subcontractor plus the quantified Cost of Quality is the true bid of that subcontractor.

Cost Plus Contract A contract that recognizes that profit is a necessary part of getting a job done. Cost plus contracts allow a profit over and above the cost involved.

Cost Review A review of the cost associated with all or part of a task or contract. Usually, but not always, cost reviews are conducted concurrently with schedule reviews and performance reviews in project, program, or division reviews.

Cost Type Contract A contract that includes cost plus provisions. The fee structure may be a percentage of cost, a fixed percentage or original bid cost, an award amount or an incentive amount. All structures are above the cost of getting the job done except that some Cost Plus Incentive Fee (CPIF) contracts have negative fee considerations as well as positive fee considerations.

Customer Meeting A meeting with the customer usually on a formal basis where an agenda and minutes are a part of the meeting. May be scheduled and required by the requirements document (contract) or may be quickly called by the customer.

Customer Relations The relations between a provider and all its customers.

Data Item Description (DID) A document consisting of a few sheets that outlines the format and requirements of a specific data report to be submitted as part of a contract. DIDs are assigned descriptive alphanumeric sequences. Originally issued to support federal government contracts, they are now more widely used.

Data Trail A documented trail that leads from a present point to a requirement point. Sometimes called a "Rabbit Trail" or "Audit Trail."

Design Review A periodic review of the design and its requirements. Typically the performer (contractor) presents and defends the design together with all supporting data. Design reviews are typically performed on an ever more detailed basis and are frequently performed on an incremental basis.

Design to Cost The cost is fixed. The design must work and meet the cost parameters.

Discrepancy Reports A report initiated to document the fact that an item under test did not meet its requirements. A Discrepancy Report must be assigned and corrected and the discrepancy must be resolved before the process can proceed.

Disposition To quantify and assign a particular action to a person or group to be completed by a specified date.

DOD The Department of Defense of the United States. Most other countries refer to this agency as the Ministry of Defense or MOD.

Dog and Pony Show A formal presentation using a lot of visual aids. Sometimes the visual aids are more compelling than the data presented.

Drop Ship To purchase materials from a vendor and have them shipped to a third location (that is, installing location or direct to the customer) without being seen at the procuring location.

Engineering Change Proposal (ECP) A proposal presented to the customer during the progress of work when a change is evidenced by events happening on the program. An ECP usually contains all the technical and cost elements of a "full blown" proposal.

Enterprise The current term for an economic unit. An enterprise may be a corporation, a company, a profit center, or cost center within a company or corporation.

Enterprise (Corporate/Company) Requirements The policies, plans, processes, and procedures at the enterprise level that drive the content of project and technical plans and the conduct of project activities.

Environment The environment contains the programmatic factors involved in producing the product. This means the safety of the workplace, the security of the workplace, and so on. It does not include product safety and security and such. These factors are technical factors.

Experience Window A tool to quickly evaluate whether or not you should bid or can perform a certain task. The principal variables are customer experience and product experience.

Farm Out To distribute with purpose.

Fast Track A method of conducting elements of a project in parallel, rather than in series, or by deleting a task, or truncating the elements of a task in terms of time or by taking a risk on one or more elements of the project to shorten the overall time involved in that element and ultimately, the project.

Fee As used in this document, fee is the same as profit—that is, the amount of money bid above cost and overhead or burden. In some specialties, such as architectural and engineering (A&E) firms and legal firms, fee has a different meaning. In these cases, fee means the money charged for doing a job. For example, an A&E firm manages the design and construction of a building. Their fee is the amount of money they charge for the service.

Financial Factors The financial policies your company has established based on law and accepted practices and dictate how your company does business.

Firm Fixed Price (FFP) A contract that is bid and awarded as a fixed amount. The customer pays a firm fixed price for some amount of work. The contractor's fee or profit is contained within that price.

First Article The first article produced by the production process. The first article is used not only to validate the design but to validate the production process as well. Sometimes the first article is delivered first, but most often, its delivery is held in abeyance, and it is used to try out improvements in design and processes. Frequently, the first article is delivered last.

Fixed Price Contract A contract in which the basic price is fixed but the fee structure can be of several different types such as Fixed Price/Incentive Fee (FP/IF), Fixed Price/Award Fee (FP/AF), and Firm Fixed Price (FFP).

Force Majeure French phrase, generally meaning an act of God, but now used as a legal term that allows recovery of costs or limits liability (depending on how written) when an act of war or superior force, such as a flood or fire, impacts the performance of the task.

Functional Manager A line manager in charge of a function such as software engineering, hardware engineering, and so on.

General and Administrative (G&A) An element of cost that generally includes the salaries of nonoperating personnel such as corporate management, human resources, finance, and so on, as well as Bid and Proposal (B&P) costs. Some companies include these costs as overhead or burden. The breakout of costs into different categories is an accounting function and is usually standardized within the type of industry in which you operate.

Give-Aways Trinkets, usually with a company logo or name, given away to advertise a product or company.

Hedge A protection against financial loss.

Hot Cutover Integrating a new element of a system into the existing system while both systems are operating.

Ilities The indirect engineering disciplines that provide Reliability, Maintainability, Availability, and so on. Also included are Health, Safety, and Environment.

Incentive Fee (IF) A fee arrangement where fee payment is based on some predetermined factors, such as schedule, quality, and cost performance. Usually awarded by the customer with concurrence by the contractor.

Incremental Testing A concept of testing that creates finished increments, so if a problem occurs, you can return to the last completed increment to fix the problem.

Independent Research and Development (IR&D) Usually an in-house **Research and Development (R&D)** program funded by the company. When the company funds this research, all results are the property of the company and are usually patented.

In-Process Review A review, frequently informal, that is conducted while a project is in process and before a major, formal review.

International Standards Organization (ISO) A worldwide federation of national standards bodies whose mission is to promote the development of international agreements that are published as International Standards.

Jabberwocky Bird A mythical bird that flew backward just to see where he had been. Introduced in a song by Phil Harris on the "Phyllis' Boyfriend" show, October 17, 1948.

Legal Factors The legal conditions existing between the program (company) and the customer and the legal conditions between the program (company) and the subcontractors or materials providers as required by law or by contractual agreement.

Lessons Learned A conference or simply a report at the end of a project to review the situations that occurred during the project and their impact on the project and how the situations could be avoided or cured in future.

Liquidated Damages An amount of money agreed to in a contract that is an estimation of damages owed to one of the parties in the event that there has been a breach by the other.

Load List The routing of a particular pin or location on a terminal board.

Materials Items where the specification is determined by the vendor. You are buying to his specification, not yours.

MIL-HDBK Military Handbook.

MIL-SPEC Military Specification.

MIL-STD Military Standard.

Mission Statement A stated action to be taken by an organization and the intended outcome of this action contained in one sentence. As an example, Abraham Lincoln's mission: to preserve the Union.

Myers-Briggs Type Indicator (MBTI) A four-character designator derived from a four-pair, eight character set resulting in sixteen combinations that represent a type of person (or later a company). Originated by Peter B. Myers and Katherine Briggs. Example: An ENTJ is an Extrovert (as opposed to an Introvert), INtuitive (as opposed to Sensing), Thinking (as opposed to Feeling), Judgmental (as opposed to Perceiving) type of person.

NASA National Aeronautics and Space Administration.

Negotiating Team An ad hoc group created to finalize the requirements for a program.

Negotiation Envelope Predetermined limit to which the Negotiating Team cannot exceed. Usually includes scope, schedule, cost, and manpower.

OCONUS Outside the Continental United States.

On-the-Job Training (OJT) Informal training provided on the job by others involved in the same category of work.

Out-of-tolerance A measured parameter that is beyond its nominal value, plus or minus a percentage of that value that is the allowable range in which that parameter may operate.

Parse To resolve or divide into component parts.

Personnel The "people" assigned to the project, the organization, and the role descriptions.

Pin Out A pin listing and its function on a terminal board, or a connector, etc.

Planning A process of intended actions that precede an event or events.

Procurement The purchasing of subcontracts and materials to be used in the output product.

Profit and Loss (P&L) The result of a contract beyond cost. A contract that returns money beyond all costs is a profit. A contract that costs more than its income is a loss.

Profit and Loss (P&L) Responsibility Responsibility assigned to a program manager for operating the program and returning a profit to the company.

Program A task external to an organization, under the aegis of a legal contract, requiring task enumeration, schedule, and cost. A program has a beginning and an ending.

Program Advisory Council A special purpose management team that advises, but does not manage, the project or program team. The Program Advisory Council acts as a transparent link between the project team and management and the customer.

Program Manager (PM) The same as a project manager, except a program manager has P&L responsibility and manages a contract with a customer outside the parent organization.

Programmatic Those issues associated with the management of a project or program. Such issues include budget, schedule, and so on. Programmatic issues are separate and distinct from technical issues.

Project Management Office (PMO) A dual-use term. 1) A centralized staff function that establishes and maintains project management processes and procedures, which does not have a line function. The APM refers to this function as the Project Support Office or PSO. 2)A major project or program office (frequently called *Big PMO*) that has other projects or programs reporting to it. In this case, the PMO has line responsibility and authority.

Project A task internal to an organization requiring task enumeration, schedule, and cost. A project has a beginning and an ending.

Project Manager (PM) The individual responsible for managing the entire project internal to the parent company.

Project Meeting A meeting, usually somewhat informal, of the entire team, where project issues are discussed.

Project Office The group of people and functions that surround the management of a project or program. These functions are usually the project manager, the administrator, the scheduler, and the secretarial function. Sometimes the chief engineer is considered as a part of the project office.

Projectized A project or program that essentially stands alone within an organization. The projectized organization contains all the line functions necessary to meet the requirements of the task or contract. Staff functions such as finance and human resources are usually not included, although they may be in extremely large projects or programs.

Proposal A presentation of a specific approach to solve a problem. In the program context it is usually an offer to do business based on a specific approach.

Prototype A nonproduction build of hardware or software generally used to test concepts, content, and interfaces. Older terms, still in use in some places, are: **Breadboard** and **Brassboard**. This term is sometimes extended to include the **First Article** of a production run. Prototypes should not be deliverable.

Purchase Order (PO) A document used to commit project, program, or company funds to a certain purchase. The PO must contain the item, the vendor, the price, and the delivery date. Other contents are at the option of the company.

Quality The project quality program, including the Quality Assurance Plan and the Quality Control Program.

Rabbit Trail A documented trail that leads from a present point to a requirement point. Sometimes called a "Data Trail" or "Audit Trail."

Ramp-Up To get started on an incremental basis.

Rapid Prototype A methodology of "build a little, test a little" rather than building the entire system.

Reengineering The common form of Business Process Management (BPM) used to establish standards for process design, deployment, execution, maintenance, and optimization.

Requirements Webster's defines requirements as something wanted or needed or something essential.

Requirements Definition Team An ad hoc group created to formalize the requirements for a project.

Requirements Flow-Down Matrix (RFM) A matrix created to track those requirements that must be flowed down to various **Work Packages**, subcontracts, and purchases. Also includes how these requirements will be flowed down. Example: Buy American Clause in a contract.

Requirements Traceability Matrix (RTM) A matrix formed to track each requirement through the lifecycle of the project. The horizontal axis of the matrix begins at project start (program award) and ends with handover. The vertical axis lists each requirement.

Research and Development (R&D) A project or program on the leading edge of technology. R&D projects can be performed in-house (see **Independent Research and Development**) or for a customer as a Research and Development program.

Resources The indirect elements necessary to support a project such as facilities and equipment. Resources are normally provided by the company, rather than the project.

Reverse Contract To take a course of contractual action and advise your customer that you intend to incorporate this change unless otherwise directed. (Be careful—some customers take a dim view of this action.)

Reverse Engineer To make a change in the specification or design and advise the customer that you intend to incorporate this change unless otherwise directed. (Be careful—some customers take a dim view of this action.)

Risk The probability that the project (programmatic risk) or the product (technical risk) will not meet some requirement while conducting the project.

Risk Mitigation Plan A plan to recognize, evaluate, and provide an approach to eliminating, mitigating, or neutralizing a technical or programmatic risk.

Root Cause The essential heart or underlying reason.

Safe Point A point or place in a process that is known to be good.

Schedule A timeline that directly supports the scope of the project.

Schedule Review A review of the schedule associated with all or part of a task or contract. Usually, but not always, schedule reviews are conducted concurrently with cost reviews and performance reviews in project, program, or division reviews.

Show Cause (Letter) An order for a company (usually a contractor or subcontractor) to tell why they think the sender (usually the customer) should not take a certain action, such as cancellation of the contract. The letter also outlines the next step that will be taken should the Show Cause not be answered.

Software Engineering Institute (SEI) The Software Engineering Institute (SEI) is a federally funded research and development center sponsored by the U.S. Department of Defense for the purpose of establishing standards and assisting others to make improvements in their software engineering capabilities.

Software Kernel An element of completed software around which other software is built.

Specification (Spec) That part of the requirements document (contract) that establishes how the system, as a whole, will perform.

Standard Requirements Reference documents common to your business area or product, such as IEEE Standards, SEI Standards, and EIA Standards that are invoked by the requirements document (contract) or the enterprise polices, plans, processes, or procedures. These standards are usually referenced rather than being reprinted simply to save space.

Statement of Work (SOW) That part of the requirements document (contract) that describes what the task is and when the task will be accomplished.

Subcontract (S/C) A contract that delegates work to a third party that contains a Statement of Work (SOW) and usually a specification.

Subcontract Requirements Traceability Matrix (SRTM) A **Requirements Traceability Matrix** (RTM) used by a subcontractor.

Subprogram Office (SPO) The SPO has the same responsibilities as the Program Office except that the SPO is responsible for only a portion of the overall system and usually does not have contractual responsibility and may not have P&L responsibility.

System Engineering Management Plan (SEMP) A top-level plan that identifies and controls the overall engineering process. The SEMP is usually supported by a number of specialty engineering plans that contain much of the engineering detail.

Targeted Selection Process A behavioral approach introduced by Development Dimensions International (DDI) that improves hiring decisions by using five basic interview principles. All interviewers work in harmony to collect and share the interview data.

Task (Challenge) See **Challenge (Tasking)**.

Team A group of people, usually interdisciplinary, brought together to perform a task. A team has a casual relationship, as opposed to **Teaming,** which denotes a legal relationship.

Team Meeting A meeting, usually somewhat informal, of the entire team where project issues are discussed.

Teaming The legal association of two or more organizations (companies) to perform a specific task. Teaming (between companies) is separate and distinct from a team (individuals).

Technical Interchange Meeting (TIM) A meeting wherein technical issues are discussed. Contractual issues are not discussed.

Tiger Team An ad hoc group formed to pursue a specific problem or issue. Their charter may be to study the issue or to find a fix or to fix it.

Total Quality Management (TQM) A structured system for meeting and exceeding internal and external customer needs and expectations by involving the entire organization in the planning and implementation of continuous and breakthrough processes improvement.

Trans Ship To purchase materials from an international location, have those materials received by your location, without import fees, and be included in the product to be shipped overseas, without export fees. This action requires considerable paperwork between all locations and governments but allows you to buy and sell materials that will be used out of your country without paying multiple import and export taxes on the materials.

Troika A Russian word meaning three. Originally intended to portray a three-horse wagon pull with the horses side-by-side. Now used in business to suggest a three-person leadership team.

Vendor A person or company that provides a product or line of products to a specification that is usually his own.

Version Description Document (VDD) A document that references and describes the changes included in this version of software.

Vision The highest view of what a company is and where it wants to go.

War Room A term first used by the military indicating a room where strategies, tactics, and general information are posted. Usually, the information is confidential, so the room is secured.

Water Cooler A common meeting place where information is exchanged. Taken from the days when every office had a water-dispensing location.

WBS See **Work Breakdown Structure**.

Work-Arounds Alternative approaches to avoid a problem or issue or situation.

Work Breakdown Structure (WBS) The presentation of the division of work to be accomplished on the project. Each element of the WBS must be costable and schedulable. The sum of the elements of the WBS is equal to the whole of the project.

Work Package (WP) The lowest level of the **WBS** that is the most efficient and cost-effective way of controlling schedule, cost, and technical performance consistent with the requirements of the customer and the performing agency (the company).

Index